JADE MARREY

A POST HILL PRESS BOOK
ISBN: 979-8-89565-680-8
ISBN (eBook): 979-8-89565-541-2

Stripped to the Soul:
A Memoir of Finding Wholeness in a Performance-Obsessed World
© 2026 by Jade Marrey
All Rights Reserved

Cover design by Jim Villaflores

This book, as well as any other Post Hill Press publications, may be purchased in bulk quantities at a special discounted rate. Contact orders@posthillpress.com for more information.

Post Hill Press
New York • Nashville
posthillpress.com

Published in the United States of America
1 2 3 4 5 6 7 8 9 10

For every woman who has ever felt like too
much and not enough at the same time.

TABLE OF CONTENTS

CHAPTER 1
PEELING BACK THE LAYERS

I never thought my life would lead me here, beneath the streets of central London, in a strip club basement that smelled of perfume and something harder to name. Desperation, maybe. But survival? Definitely. As I stood under the fluorescent lights, heart racing, I realized this wasn't just another night. It was the start of something I didn't yet understand. Peeling back each layer of clothing was a daring act of faith, exposing not just my skin but the very essence of who I was. My heart was racing, but I kept my face calm, my movements smooth, so that no one would guess what was going on inside. Despite the fear, as I danced, a spark lit somewhere deep inside me—something ancient, untamed, and hungry to be remembered.

This career shocked not only me but also Harry, my boyfriend. When I mustered the courage to reveal my profession, he looked at me with a mix of disbelief and something darker, his reaction activating wounds I had long tried to conceal from the world, and from him.

"A stripper?" His voice was tight, betraying more than just surprise.

Was it judgment, disappointment, or perhaps a flicker of morbid curiosity? I was familiar with all three. The question hung between us, loaded with unspoken implications. I knew his question wasn't just about how I found the job. It was about the path that had led me here, the desperation or desire that drove me to bare not just my body but pieces of my soul to strangers, night after night. I could see his mind racing, struggling to piece together the fragments of who I was versus the image of the person he thought he had come to know during our time together.

I felt the change in him in that moment and wondered if this would be the beginning of the end for us. The initial excitement of our new relationship was now overshadowed by the enormity of my truth. I could see the struggle in his eyes, reflecting a new dimension to our connection, one filled with uncertainty. His gaze, filled with unspoken questions, sought answers I didn't yet have myself.

Even now, those who meet me are intrigued when they hear about my past and curious about the transformation that led me to who I am today. I can feel the shift in their demeanor when I reveal my past profession. Suddenly they lean in, eyes sharp, craving the gory details. The path of a stripper was never one I envisioned for myself.

But do any of us truly know what life has in store?

Is our journey a co-creation with some greater force, or is it predestined, each situation meticulously placed for the evolution of our soul? These questions lingered in my mind, as enigmatic as the flashing neon signs that became the backdrop to my metamorphosis.

The hidden, unspoken world in the private room of the club became my unlikely crucible of self-discovery. Who could have foreseen that the path to understanding my soul would be paved with lipstick and lace? Or the click of stilettos on hardwood forming the rhythm of my personal enlightenment?

Yet there I was, some kind of accidental philosopher in a world where fantasy and reality blurred—just like the vision of a man on his third drink.

The great cosmic mystery that guided my path seemed beyond comprehension, a life I couldn't make sense of yet. It was as if I had stumbled into a realm where the laws of reality bent and shifted, a place where the boundaries between the mundane and the mystical merged.

It felt spiritual, even if no one would call it that.

Little did I know that this self-imposed exile would lead me straight into a world where detachment was currency. The strip club, with its seductive illusions of intimacy and its transient connections, became a perfect mirror to the pattern I had unconsciously made my existence. As I twirled around the polished pole, I couldn't shake the feeling that I was dancing not just for the crowd, but for answers to questions I didn't even know how to articulate.

Yet, as I delved deeper into the unknown, I started to meet parts of myself that I never knew existed: the seductress, the therapist, the actress.

They were all me, all aspects of the feminine that I was only beginning to understand. What other wonders lie hidden within me, waiting to be uncovered? What other sides of being a woman were waiting for me to meet them?

The spotlight beat down on me, its heat merging with anticipation under my skin. Before me, a sea of hungry eyes gazed up. Yet as I looked down at them, a strange calm descended.

Any fear I previously felt had lifted. I was laid bare, in nothing but a pair of clear heels and skin shimmering under the lights. But as I moved across the stage, I understood that what they saw was more than just my body.

Each step, each measured sway of my hips, told a story—my story—unfolding before them. The audience, though they didn't know it, had entered into an unspoken agreement with me, one I had forged within myself long before stepping onto the stage.

"What's your name, sweetheart?"

He was slouched in a rumpled suit, eyes glazed with the kind of weariness alcohol only deepened.

I tilted my head, smile polished, voice sweet. "Whatever you want it to be."

His chuckle was low, hollow. I watched him fumble for charm but slip into something closer to sorrow.

For a moment, it wasn't a stage. It was two ghosts sharing a glance in a room built on forgetting.

As I watched him closely, I noticed the way his shoulders sagged under the weight of unspoken burdens, his smile not quite reaching his eyes.

I may have been wearing a mask that night, but he too wore a mask and struggled to maintain an air of charm while hiding the sadness that threatened to break through. My heart ached for him, a fleeting connection forming in that underground club.

I caught myself wondering what stories lay behind the feigned confidence, the inner demons that no one could see, and what dreams had slipped through his fingers. I traded my identity for a fantasy story that I would live vicariously through to get the outcome I needed, creating personas like costumes: the girl next door, the femme fatale, and the damsel in distress, which was my personal favorite.

The irony wasn't lost on me that this nightly ritual mirrored the lives of so many beyond the club's walls, their own masks perhaps less glittery but no less present.

How many people wear unconscious disguises as they leave their homes each morning?

We wear suits like armor. Curate our feeds like movie characters. Tell stories to strangers we'll never meet again, all in pursuit of being seen in a certain light. Is it ego that drives us, or a primal yearning to be accepted, chosen, as if our very survival depends on it? (It often does, emotionally.)

Perhaps we're all trying to survive in our own ways, attempting to escape our realities by losing ourselves in carefully curated illusions that promise everything we desire, only to leave us feeling emptier and more resentful of the truth we've left behind, like a hangover after a night of cheap champagne.

The strip club was a microcosm of the world we navigate: unpredictable, thrilling, and often unforgiving. It provided a semblance of what I thought I needed: financial security, a sense of empowerment, and an illusion of control. Yet paradoxically, I found myself at the mercy of circumstances I couldn't predict, grappling with resentment and the dawning realization that there's a dark side to control, a way in which we become enslaved to systems of our making, be it the dazzling matrix of the club or the mundane routine of everyday life.

This duality became a constant companion, challenging my perceptions and pushing me to look beyond the surface, revealing the raw humanity and pain beneath.

In a way, we are all engaging in the act of stripping.

As we forge connections with others, we engage in a delicate dance of revelation, slowly peeling back the layers of our soul like a dancer teasing her audience. There's an art to this personal unveiling, one that I mastered as a self-protective measure in a career that most people would not understand. It involves a careful curation of which parts to show and which to keep hidden, reserving the most sensitive secrets for those who demonstrate a genuine interest in our lives. The act of revealing yourself to another person is an interplay of vulnerability and self-preservation, a game of emotions where we calculate how much to give without risking it all. It's a leap of faith to show your weakness to someone else, to place yourself at the mercy of another with those oh-so-vulnerable words: "Please stay a little longer" or, "Help me. I really need you."

In our modern society, the ease with which we offer our bodies to strangers stands in stark contrast to the fear we feel at the prospect of baring our souls. That fear, rooted in abandonment wounds or attachment anxiety, is more universal than we admit.

I first realized this on a slow Tuesday night shift while confiding in a fellow dancer.

"You know," I said, almost laughing, "sometimes I think it's easier to take off my clothes than to let someone know the real truth."

She nodded without hesitation. We both knew what I meant.

The memory of my own words haunted me, because in this reluctance to fully reveal ourselves, aren't we abandoning the very essence of who we are?

If we grew up feeling unseen or rejected, we often fear that real intimacy will cost us something. We perform. We shrink. We hide the bits that feel most like us. Our society, as well as our own fears, teaches us to reject parts of our story. We tuck them away in dark corners like crumpled cash. But what if we could do the opposite? What if we could gather every shard of ourselves, every memory, mistake, and masked version, and offer it up without apology? What would our world look like if we didn't feel compelled to play these roles to be admired? If we stopped trying to survive intimacy and instead let it change us? To be seen—really seen—takes more than stage lights. It takes nerve and a kind of nakedness no costume can fake. And that's why this story begins here.

Not because this is about stripping, but because it's about choosing to be known anyway.

Even when it's uncomfortable.

Even when it costs you everything you once used to feel safe.

Because the real performance?

Is learning to live without the mask.

CHAPTER 2
FAMILY AFFAIRS

I was five when I first realized my family didn't look like other people's. My life was always a bit different. Full of contrasts—joy and sorrow, shadow and light. Definitely not what most people would call "normal." I was born into a fractured household, where love and pain coexisted in a delicate, uneasy balance. The cracks in my family were not always visible, but I felt them, sensed them, even before I understood their origins. Other kids talked about dads as if they were fixtures in the home, like TVs or dinner tables. Mine was a question mark. I grew up in Ellesmere Port, a small industrial town in the northwest of England, where rows of council estates stood shoulder to shoulder under gray skies, and everything—from the pavement to the people—seemed a little tired, a little worn. It was the kind of place where stories went unspoken and grief was passed down like an inheritance. Years later, I would come to learn the truth behind my family's fractures: a turbulent love affair between two souls, each bearing their own invisible scars, both searching for something they couldn't find in each other.

My father, a man I knew only through whispered stories and faded photographs, was a phantom in my life. I learned from my mother, in time, that he had fled from the suffocating embrace of shame and inadequacy, a specter that haunted him more than any physical poverty ever could. I think he felt, like a lot of men do, that if he couldn't be the provider, he wasn't enough. That he was failing us by staying. He told himself that, by leaving, he was protecting me from a life of hardship, but to the little girl left behind, it felt like betrayal. His absence carved a void in my heart, echoing with the unspoken question: Was I not enough to make him stay? I searched for him in places he would never be, in faces that would never quite match his, in the arms of men who could never fill the space he left behind. And perhaps, in some ways, I am still searching.

That abandonment left a mark, like scar tissue wrapped around my heart. I learned, perhaps too young, that love was not something you could count on, that people left without warning and without looking back. Even now I can still feel the silence of our Ellesmere Port kitchen pressing in on me, the invisible pressure of everything left unsaid. As a result, I kept others at arm's length, building walls of indifference brick by careful brick, my defenses as intricate as they were invisible. Life became a complex dance of push and pull, allowing people close enough to glimpse a fragment of my true self, but never near enough to truly touch my soul. If they couldn't reach me, they couldn't hurt me when they inevitably left.

That first club I worked at in central London couldn't have been more different from where I grew up. The gray skies and cracked pavements were still there, but inside, the club shimmered with wealth and illusion—velvet walls, diamond chokers, men in tailored suits ordering magnums of champagne like water. It felt like another universe compared to our narrow, terraced two-up two-down at the edge of the port, where the wallpaper curled at the corners and nothing ever really felt new. Inside the club, everything was curated to feel expensive and powerful, and for a while, I believed stepping into that world meant stepping into control. Each performance became a ritual, a desperate attempt to exorcise the ghosts of my past while unknowingly summoning souls that would change the course of my future.

In this twilight world, I found an unexpected kinship with the lonely souls who sought solace in the temporary fantasy we provided. We were all running from something, all hiding behind carefully crafted personas, seeking connection in the only way we knew how to. The men who came looking for escape weren't so different from the women who gave it to them. But as the weeks turned into months, a nagging question took root in my mind: Was I truly protecting myself, or was I merely constructing an elaborate cage of my own design? The answer, I suspected, lay hidden somewhere between the twenty-pound bills and the discarded dreams that littered the club's floor each night—some crumpled, some damp with spilled vodka, the edges sticking to your stilettos as you walked.

My mother, bless her wounded heart, tried to be both nurturing warmth and guiding light, but performing the dual roles of mother and father often proved too heavy, and she found solace in the bottom of wine bottles. The rich, burgundy liquid became her escape, leaving me to navigate the choppy waters of childhood largely alone. I learned early on that parents are not always protectors, that sometimes the people who are meant to keep you safe are the ones who teach you how to survive instead. This paradoxical upbringing—devoid of masculine guidance and yearning for true maternal nurturing—forged me into a woman of steel and silk. On the surface, I was unbreakable, a force to be reckoned with. But beneath that hardened exterior lay a little girl still crying out for the love she never received.

When I was little, I'd disappear into my imagination. In that world, my mum laughed easily and life felt like one of those storybooks with happy endings. Perhaps it was this early retreat into imagination that sharpened my sensitivity to the unspoken. I was blessed—or perhaps cursed—with a profound empathy that allowed me to sense the emotions of others, to read between the lines of what people said and what they truly meant. This gift, as I would later discover, was a double-edged sword, a priceless skill that would serve me well in the game of adulthood and enable me to deftly navigate the intricate dance of human interaction. It also meant I felt too much, absorbed too much, often at the expense of my own peace.

Those long car rides through the Irish countryside became the backdrop to my wandering thoughts. I'd press my forehead to the cool glass, tracing the fog with my fingertip, watching emerald fields roll by like waves. The stone walls blurred into memory, the sheep-flecked hills oblivious to the tension tightening the air inside our car. Sometimes there was only silence—thick, heavy, unspoken. Other times it was louder: slamming fists, trembling sobs, threats flung like gravel against the windscreen. Even the beauty of the road couldn't drown the violence of what it carried.

This same empathy, born from the need to interpret my mother's unpredictable moods and the tense silences of our home, became both a shield and a survival tactic. I learned to anticipate the emotional storms, to hear the edge in her voice before it became a shout, to see the weariness in her eyes before it turned to frustration and brace myself for the inevitable crashes of despair, anger, and distance. What began as an instinct for self-preservation during my childhood soon became a vital skill in my adult life—especially in the unpredictable atmosphere of the strip club. Yet it also deepened my connection with others, offering me a rare ability to relate to people on a more human level and feel the world in ways that others couldn't.

Now, with the wisdom of years, I find compassion softening the edges of understanding when I think of my mum, Adele. How arduous a task it must have been to raise three children alone when she herself was barely treading water and trying not to drown. To survive, she sold herself in a different way than I would come to do—to the corporate rat race, a relentless grind that promised the safety she had long craved as a child but never fully experienced. Born to a mentally ill mother and an emotionally absent father, a family that functioned in name only. Her youth was spent pushing back against a system that had failed her, her rebellion as fierce as her longing for love. The weight of her unfulfilled childhood dreams hung heavy on her shoulders, breeding a resentment toward her dysfunctional family that sent her seeking freedom on wide-open roads at full throttle. The roar of her Harley became a battle cry as she drove as far as possible from the life she knew, leaving behind a trail of broken expectations and unspoken pain. It's only now that I can look back and see not just what she failed to give me, but what she gave me without knowing—tenacity, rebellion, and a hunger for something more.

It's a cruel trick of fate how, despite our best efforts, we often unknowingly follow the very patterns we swore we would never repeat. How we attract partners who mirror the wounds of our parents or find ourselves making choices shaped by the experiences we fought to outrun. For Adele, sex, drugs, and rock and roll became her refuge, an antidote to numb her reality. That is, until the day her world collided with my father's and fate delivered an unexpected plot twist—a little, unplanned, but life-altering "mistake"—me.

My mother, ever the optimist despite her hardships, believed that the news of her pregnancy would be the catalyst for change in Dave, my father. She clung to this hope with both hands, convinced a child would awaken a sense of responsibility in him, a reason to stay and finally choose family over substances. Even as evidence to the contrary mounted, she held onto that belief like a lifeline. "He's still here, Adele," the barmaid would shout down the phone, her voice barely audible over the cacophony of another rowdy night at the local pub. There he was again, my father, out at the pub instead of at home with us, numbing himself with alcohol, either searching for the elusive meaning of life or desperately trying to forget it altogether.

But Adele was never one to play the role of the long-suffering woman. Fiery and untamed, she finally decided she had had enough. Fueled by a potent mix of disappointment, anger, and fierce instinct to protect her child, she stormed into the night to confront him. What happened next would become legend in my family—a story passed down with pain and pride. The ensuing altercation left a broken door in its wake as my mother delivered the final blow and left my father nursing a bloodied nose. In that moment of violence and anguish, my almost-family shattered into irreparable pieces. What should have been the foundation of my early life instead became a complex chronicle of trauma and a survival guide all in one. My mother had fought for me before I had even taken my first breath, and as I would later come to understand, that was both the first and last time she ever fought for him.

As I reminisce about these extracts of my family's history, I'm struck by the intricate web of emotions that binds us all together. The legacy of pain, hope, and resilience that courses through my veins is both a burden and a source of strength. It's a reminder that our stories are never simply our own but rather a continuation of those who came before us. Their dreams, their failures, and their unwavering determination to survive shape us in ways I am still uncovering. In the quiet moments, when the weight of my own choices presses heavily upon me, I often wonder: How much of my mother's fire burns within me? How much of my father's restlessness? And how deeply have their struggles imprinted themselves into my very being?

My father's relentless pursuit of freedom from his own mind, a trait I've come to recognize in myself, is a complex inheritance. It manifests as an irrepressible urge to break free from constraints, to seek open spaces and endless possibilities. This yearning for autonomy drives me to challenge boundaries, to resist the comfortable confines of convention, and to forge my own path in life. I see it in the way I approach relationships, in my career choices, in my hunger for reinvention, in the restless itch that has pulled me from city to city, chapter to chapter. Like him, I find myself drawn to the promise of escape, the allure of a fresh start. But unlike him, I'm learning to take that same yearning and channel it into something more sustainable, creating a life that honors my need for independence while also nurturing the relationships and responsibilities that give my life meaning rather than a reason to run. My father spent his life searching for an exit, but I am determined to create something worth staying for.

My mother's fire, on the other hand, manifests as fierce determination, a refusal to be beaten down by life's hardships despite the odds. It's the spark that ignites when I'm faced with adversity, the inner voice that urges me to get back up. When provoked, this inherited temper flares up with an intensity that can be both awe-inspiring and terrifying. It's a blaze that can illuminate injustices and fuel righteous anger, driving me to stand up against wrongs and fight for what I believe in. But it's also a fire that, if left unchecked, can burn down everything in its path, leaving behind a trail of scorched earth and damaged relationships.

I've seen this fire ignite in moments of frustration before I could control it, burning away reason and restraint. Words become weapons, sharp and cutting, capable of inflicting deep wounds that linger long after the flames of anger have subsided. In these moments, I recognize the echo of my mother's voice in my own, the same intensity, the same capacity to strike fear or awe in those around me. But as I grow, I'm learning that this fire does not always have to destroy. When wielded with awareness, it can be a powerful force for change, illuminating instead of incinerating. This fire is what fuels my passion, drives my ambition, and gives me the courage to stand up for what I believe in. I'm constantly working to find balance as I carry this fire with me. I'm learning to recognize the early sparks and take a breath before the inferno ignites. I'm discovering that it's possible to feel deeply, to burn with conviction, without reducing everything around me to cinders. It's not something I want to suppress, but to direct, because it's a part of who I am, a testament to the passion and strength that runs in my blood. And perhaps that's the deeper truth I've come to understand—not just that I've inherited trauma, but that I've inherited tools. Pain shaped me, yes, but so did resistance. So did choice.

It was this dichotomy between the inheritance from my father and mother—the desire to push boundaries coupled with fierce determination—that gave me the audacity to push open those heavy club doors and step into a world that both terrified and enticed me. The absence of a safety net, of a supportive family to fall back on, had inadvertently gifted me both desperation and determination, much like my mum before me. I had no one to catch me if I fell, so I learned to fly on my own, even if my wings were built from uncertainty and survival. Even as I acknowledge the circumstances that led me there, a lingering mystery tugs at the edges of my mind. What unseen force whispered in my ear, urging me to buy that first pair of clear heels? What cosmic string was pulled to guide me toward that initial pole-dancing class? Was it fate, free will, or some deeper calling buried within me?

Little did I know, unraveling these mysteries would force me to confront not only my family's secrets but also the parts of myself I'd kept hidden for so long. The pain of my past was the chisel that cracked me open, revealing potential I had never dared to believe in. And here's the truth I came to understand, not in a therapist's office but under club lights, in dressing rooms, and through a hundred mirrored glances at myself in the dark: The things we carry from childhood shape everything. Our need to be loved. Our fear of being left. The little roles we learn to play so we can feel safe in a world that doesn't always make sense.

They call it "attachment theory," but let me say it how I lived it: *If you grow up never knowing when love might disappear, you learn to be prepared.* You learn to perform. You learn to shrink or shine, depending on who's watching. That's why I didn't just end up a stripper. I became a woman who knew how to be loved in fragments. In fantasy. In pieces. One lap dance at a time. Always giving enough to be wanted, never enough to be truly known. Because that was safer. That was familiar.

But somewhere along the line, survival stopped being enough. I didn't want to just protect myself. I wanted to understand myself.

I didn't want to keep reenacting old wounds in new outfits. I wanted to live a life where I could finally be whole. Not a curated version of me, not the girl who wore masks better than most—but me. All of me.

This journey became more than just one of survival. It became one of unearthing long-buried secrets, of bridging the divide of twenty-nine years to reconnect with shadows of myself and my family that were long ago abandoned. It was terrifying, exhilarating, and profoundly transformative.

Somewhere in that process, I began to ask different questions. Not just, "Why did they hurt me?" but, "What did I learn about love from that pain?" Not just, "What did I lose?" but, "What did I become because of it?"

Now, I invite you to consider a perspective that might seem radical at first glance. What if we chose our parents? What if, on some cosmic plane, our souls handpicked the perfect storms, the exact tribulations, and the precise relationships needed to shape us into who we were meant to become? It's a perspective that challenges our notions of victimhood and destiny, but it also begs a deeper question. If we chose this life, with all its pain and beauty, what greater purpose could we be preparing for?

We often cling to the "what ifs" and "if onlys" of our past, but what if the person who left you, who wrongfully abandoned you, was also sparing you from a deeper pain their limitations would have eventually caused? What if the life you grieved and so desperately wanted had led you astray from your true path? I'm suggesting a radical shift in perspective. See every moment of your life, every joy and heartbreak, as a stepping stone leading you to your higher self. When we embrace this view, something powerful happens. We can begin to release the white-knuckled grip we have on our past hurts. We can exhale the grief we've held in our hearts like heirlooms through generations. We stop waiting for an apology that may never come. Instead, we reclaim our power and inhale the possibilities of the present moment.

This isn't about dismissing the pain or minimizing the struggles. It's about finding meaning in the madness, purpose in the pain. Because the truth is, I didn't just inherit wounds. I inherited wisdom. I didn't just absorb fear. I also absorbed fire. My story isn't a tragedy. It's a training ground. And every lesson, every heartbreak, every ache in my chest was teaching me how to come home to myself.

That's what this chapter was really about. Not the strip club. Not the abandonment. But the journey back to wholeness. To remembering that even when we're broken open, we're never beyond repair.

And that realization, my dear reader, is the first step on the path to true freedom.

CHAPTER 3

HITTING ROCK BOTTOM

It was one of those damp, gray afternoons on the King's Road, the kind where the wind cuts right through your coat. I dragged my feet past shop windows I couldn't afford to step into, each step heavier than the last, as if I were walking through the ruins of a life I had once believed in. The retail job that had previously given me purpose, structure, and the independence of earning my own way had felt like a lifeline. Now it felt like a noose tightening around my neck, each shift draining me rather than saving me.

The sense of hopelessness was a familiar weight, one I had grown accustomed to while sleeping on a friend's sofa, desperately calculating how much more I needed to save before I could afford a place of my own. My previous rented room in a shared studio apartment, with its missing windowpanes and doors that refused to close properly, had left me grappling with the choice between an unstable living situation and a genuine threat to my safety. Leaving was not just an option; it was a necessity.

One night, as I walked through the darkened council estate, an unsettling presence seemed to follow me. The quiet of the streets grew heavier, and every sound felt amplified. For a few minutes, I forced myself to walk at a measured pace, even though my heart was beating out of my chest. I told myself that running might just escalate the situation—I should remain calm. Then, in an instant, the fear took on cosmic proportions, as if the universe was issuing a stark wake-up call, warning me of imminent danger. It was a primal, undeniable signal that compelled me to act swiftly. I rushed home. That night, as I lay in my tiny, cold room, staring at the cracked ceiling, I knew I had to make a change. With the clarity that only fear can bring, I gathered what little I had and moved into a friend's living room for the foreseeable future. Though this temporary refuge offered a small comfort, it underscored a larger truth: I feared for my life, both physically and existentially.

As I grappled with the disorienting chaos of my life, I felt like Alice, tumbling down a rabbit hole of my own making. I was desperately searching for myself amid the bright, deceptive city lights of underground raves and the chemical haze of superficial encounters. I'd find solace with coked-up London finance boys who had more money than sense. Their designer suits and inflated egos provided a brief escape, a fleeting illusion of the glamorous life I thought I desired. Yet, as dawn broke and the high faded, I was left staring at my own reflection in bathroom mirrors with the bitter aftertaste of regret, a void that no amount of drugs could fill. The city that once promised so much now felt like a maze of night buses, dead-end jobs, and mornings I couldn't remember.

Weeks stretched into a continuous blur of work and wild nights, my attempts to both escape and rebuild my life merging into one chaotic experience. My memories of those nights are fragmented, like brief flashes of light in an otherwise dark expanse. London had become both my playground and my prison. Eventually, I managed to find a small room in the basement of a Victorian house just off Tottenham Court Road. The front door stuck in damp weather, and the hallway smelled faintly of old takeaway boxes. But it was mine. The space was tiny, just enough for a single bed and a wardrobe, but it was a personal refuge, a small victory in a long battle. Just as I began to believe that I might be turning a corner, reality reminded me of its persistent grip.

One morning, as I dragged myself into work from a club, Susie, my manager, pulled me aside. Her eyes, usually keen and businesslike, softened with an unexpected concern that left me feeling vulnerable. "Maybe it's time to hand in your notice. Take care of yourself."

I laughed it off, but her words hit me in the gut. I was drowning, and everyone could see it but me.

My once boundless enthusiasm had faded, replaced by a hollow imitation of the vibrant personality that had once been my greatest asset. The structure of my job kept me afloat, but on my days off, a void yawned, and I frantically tried to fill it, creating a downward spiral of chaos that was now threatening to upend my entire life. My sporadic days off felt like landmines scattered across my schedule, each absence a silent cry for help that I struggled to articulate. "Fake it till you make it," the mantra of survival in this cutthroat city. But how long could one fake it before the mask became too heavy to bear? I owed so much to my personality, that effervescent charm that had opened doors and won people over. Without it, I wouldn't be here right now. But where exactly was "here"? And was it where I truly wanted to be?

As a child, people would approach my single, struggling mother, their eyes alight with the promise they saw in me. "That girl should be on stage," they'd say, watching me twirl in grocery store aisles, my laughter too big for the space I was in. "She'll go far in life, mark my words." Their prophetic words lingered in my mind as I faced failure head-on. Why did my life feel like the antithesis of the success they imagined for me? Why couldn't I see the spark that others had so confidently predicted?

Now, to explain something I've learned along the way: The way we feel about ourselves often comes from deep patterns formed over time—like invisible programming running in the background of our minds. These patterns don't just affect our thoughts; they shape how we respond to challenges and opportunities. Sometimes, they keep us stuck in familiar but unhealthy cycles because stepping outside them feels risky or unknown. Understanding this helps us realize that change isn't just about trying harder but about gently reprogramming these hidden habits of thought.

Reflecting on the prophetic words of my childhood, I realized the irony wasn't lost on me. I did end up on stage and achieved more than I ever thought possible. However, pride is a fickle thing, easily weighed down by self-doubt and a gnawing sense of inadequacy. We are often our own worst enemies, limiting our potential through a lack of self-worth or confidence. Our internal beliefs can imprison us, confining us to what we feel we deserve rather than what we might achieve.

Society's metrics for success—status, wealth, profession, and the carefully curated image we project—can be merciless and unforgiving. But what if we've been measuring success all wrong? What if true success lies not in these external validations but in who we are at our core? What if our achievements are merely bonuses, the cherry on top of the sundae of our authentic selves? And perhaps most crucially, what if the real measure of success is not in what we accumulate for ourselves but in how we use our gifts to enrich the lives of others?

I didn't know it then, but I know it now: True success should be a reflection of personal growth and fulfillment, found in the joy of simple moments and meaningful connections. It's about waking up with a sense of purpose and going to bed with a sense of peace. It's about living authentically, aligned with your values, and making a positive impact on those around you. If you're searching for a glimmer of hope amid the darkness of self-doubt, try to view your struggles as an opportunity to redefine success on your own terms. Success is not a destination. It comes from a deep inner knowing about living authentically, growing into your fullest expression of yourself, and making the world a little brighter simply by being in it.

As I emerged from the tube station one night in early September, the street was wet, reflecting streaks of neon. That's when I saw it, the Gentlemen's Club sign glowing against the dusk, like it had been waiting for me all along. I'd passed it a hundred times before, but tonight, it seemed to lure me in with possibility. I was still limping along at my retail job, but I knew I wasn't going to be there much longer. My small room that I called home was a refuge, but I was still drowning. My gaze locked with the bouncer's—a towering figure with a weathered face that hinted at countless stories and hard-won wisdom. His name tag read Mike, and his presence exuded a no-nonsense air that spoke of experience rather than harshness. In that moment, a strange calm settled over me, as if the universe had finally decided to throw me a lifeline.

My nails gleamed a defiant crimson under the harsh street-lights, freshly manicured as if in preparation for this very moment. As I stood there, riveted by the sign, I remembered that in the depths of my closet lay a pair of stripper heels, purchased on a whim for the pole-dancing classes I'd been attending for fun in a dimly lit studio tucked away in the sketchy streets of East London. Those classes had been an escape, a rebellion against the mundane, but now they seemed like a prophecy fulfilled. It was as if all the random pieces of my life were suddenly falling into place, forming a picture I'd never painted in my mind.

As I stood there on the precipice of a life-altering decision, I couldn't help but ponder what cosmic alignment had conspired to open my eyes at this precise moment and how many times I had walked this very path, unaware of the sign that had always been there, a silent sentinel watching my daily commute.

I lay in bed that night in my tiny basement room near Euston Station. The rhythmic rattle of passing trains, once an irritation, now seemed like a countdown, urging me toward…what? Salvation? Damnation? The line between the two had never felt so faint, but I couldn't help but wonder: Was this desperation or destiny? I thought of the words I had heard so often as a child: "That girl belongs on a stage." I almost laughed at the irony. They had been right. Just not in the way anyone had ever imagined.

And then, as the first light of the morning crept through the window, I realized rock bottom wasn't just a place of despair. And it wasn't somewhere I had to stay—it was a crossroads. I could continue to stare into the gutter, lost in the wreckage of what could have been, and let the city swallow me whole, or I could look up at the vast expanse of infinite possibilities stretching out before me like the night sky, as boundless and bewildering as the great cosmic mystery that surrounds us all—ever-changing, and omnipresent.

Our choices are not casual things that can be quickly explained but intricate reflections of our inner world. Each choice we make has a complex origin and is motivated by a tangle of thoughts and emotions that shape how we interact with our very reality, unspoken fears, and deeply ingrained beliefs. Our actions are shaped by the stories we tell ourselves, by the wounds we carry, and by the silent, persistent longing for something more. This is why the journey of introspection is so important. It is through peeling back the layers of our psyche that we begin to unravel the complex patterns and beliefs that have long dictated our lives. It is only through this courageous act of self-discovery that we can consciously reclaim choice and move toward the vision we hold for our lives, each step a deliberate stride toward our dreams and a rebellion against all the things that held us back.

But how does one navigate this journey of self-realization? The answer lies in two equally powerful forces: an unwavering clarity of purpose and the mysterious whispers of intuition. To move forward with intention, we must see the path ahead. We must dare to dream, to envision the destination before we take the first step. When I saw the neon sign of the club, it was as if a hidden part of me had already made the decision before my conscious mind could catch up, revealing something I hadn't even realized I was searching for. Suddenly, I knew I had a choice, and I began to envision the things a job like that could provide me: much-needed money, which would give me the security and the stability I'd never had in my life. At the same time, for those who find themselves lost in the fog of uncertainty, clarity can feel impossibly distant. In these moments, when logic and planning fail, another path exists—one that requires us to attune ourselves to the subtle frequencies of our inner voice, allowing that ethereal guide to illuminate the way forward. And perhaps that is the great paradox of self-discovery: We don't always know what we are looking for until we find it.

However, that inner voice is not infallible. It's a tool, but like any tool, it requires careful tuning. Our intuition, though powerful, is not always an unerring compass pointing due north. It can be thrown off course by the pull of past traumas and the gravitational force of outdated belief systems. These deceptive influences act as cosmic interference, distorting the guidance from our highest self and obscuring the downloads of greater wisdom that seek to reach us from beyond the veil of ordinary consciousness. To trust oneself fully is not just about listening to intuition but discerning when that voice is speaking from truth and when it is whispering from fear.

The hero's journey of self-discovery is not for the faint of heart. It demands that we challenge everything we think we know and embark on a task of unlearning and reprogramming our minds. This pilgrimage of the soul requires us to confront our deepest fears and shatter the illusions that have long held us captive. It demands that we step beyond the narratives we inherited that define our worth by the expectation of others and reclaim the pen to write our own. Only then can we hope to relinquish control from the iron grip of our subconscious and ego.

I made the decision to pursue self-discovery that night, looking at the Gentlemen's Club sign. I realized all too clearly that my life had become something I did not want; I was making decisions that didn't serve me and seeking to waste the time I had in distractions to ease my pain, rather than spending my energy investing in something I could build, something that would move me forward. Though I didn't realize it at the time, this decision was born not just out of necessity but a touch of madness, and it would unlock parts of myself I had yet to discover. The journey ahead promised to challenge everything I thought I knew about life, love, and my own resilience. This unexpected turn was not merely about achieving financial stability; it was a gateway to a deeper understanding of myself and my place in the world. By stepping into the unknown, I would be compelled to dismantle the constructs of my identity—those fragile illusions of self-worth and purpose built on societal expectations and personal fears. What seemed like an irrational choice was, in fact, a catalyst for a profound philosophical and spiritual awakening.

The next day, I arrived for an audition in the mid-afternoon. As I reached for the door handle, my fingers trembling slightly, I couldn't shake the feeling that I was stepping into a story that had been waiting for me all along. Deep down, somehow, inexplicably, I knew I was exactly where I needed to be. As I slowly descended the stairs, the thrum of bass vibrated through my bones. I reached the last step into a new chapter of my life—one that promised to be as challenging as it was transformative.

CHAPTER 4
EVERYTHING HAS A PRICE

"Have you danced before?" she asked, her tone dripping with skepticism. A curvaceous Eastern European woman with pencil-thin, tattooed eyebrows and a waist to match eyed me with a mixture of curiosity and disbelief. Her stare seemed to pierce through my facade, as if she could sense the uncertainty lurking beneath my forced smile.

"I can dance," I said, trying to keep my voice steady. I injected as much confidence into those three words as I could, hoping they would compensate for the way my hands clenched at my sides. It was a bluff, of course. One I hoped she wouldn't call.

The truth was, I had never set foot inside a strip club, let alone worked in one. My knowledge of what was expected of me extended no further than pop culture clichés and a handful of pole-dancing classes taken on a whim. The idea of taking my clothes off in front of strangers was something I had compartmentalized, filed away in the part of my brain that refused to think too deeply about what I was walking into. If I thought too much, I'd run.

"Okay. Come on back," she said with an air of mild disinterest, her sigh suggesting she had seen plenty of girls like me before. Fresh meat. Wide-eyed. Unaware of the choices we were about to make just by existing in a space we didn't yet understand. My heart raced as she ushered me down a narrow corridor into the changing room, a liminal space, a portal between my old life and the uncertain future that awaited me. The changing room, tucked behind the club's main floor, smelled of hairspray and stale perfume. I took it all in. The cluttered countertops lined with half-empty lipsticks and cheap eyelash glue, the crumpled pound bills stuffed into open bags, the discarded stilettos strewn across the floor like remnants of a battle long fought.

As I slipped on the delicate lingerie and gown I'd shopped for earlier that day, and the towering heels I'd retrieved from the back of my closet, I felt like an actress preparing for the performance of a lifetime. The stage manager, a young English lad with an air of detached efficiency, had given me a quick rundown before I came to the dressing room. His instructions replayed in my mind like a mantra: *Enter stage right when the music starts, and be confident.* Little did I know that the songs that would play tonight would become the soundtrack to a chapter of my life filled with experiences beyond my wildest imagination. And later, those same songs would haunt me, looping endlessly, tethered to memories that would leave me questioning everything— love, power, even the very purpose of existence.

I finished getting dressed, readjusting the neckline of my gown and giving my hair one more shake. I reassured myself that I did indeed know how to dance, and how hard could taking your clothes off be? After all, I had done it countless times for forgotten strangers in past romances. But as I stood there, trembling slightly in my new attire, I realized that this was different. This man, whom I would later learn was my boss, stood between me and my chance at survival. The next two minutes of my life would bear the weight of my future as I bid farewell to my past.

The routine was simple yet fraught with significance: Begin fully dressed in a gown, then strip down to bra and thong, and for the grand finale, remove the bra. These direct instructions were all I had to go on, and I was determined to give it my all. I knew it wouldn't always be this simple—that the more complex, true rules of survival in this new world would reveal themselves in time—but this first night, all I had were those three simple steps. With each layer I stripped away, it felt as though I was shedding an old identity, the memories of every missed opportunity and every abandoned dream dissolving into the dim lights, replaced by the woman I would become in order to survive.

Once the lights went down and the last notes of the song faded into the ether, I picked my pride up from the floor along with my discarded clothing and entered a realm that seemed distorted from reality yet made perfect sense in its own twisted way. The dressing room now buzzed with activity as dancers prepared for what felt like an impending battle. I still wasn't sure if I'd passed the audition, if I had the job or not. Rows of lockers stood in military formation, and perfectly lit mirrors reflected an army of women in various stages of transformation. The racks of costumes overflowed with lace, sequins, and silk, each piece offering the possibility for reinvention. I hoped I would get the chance to choose from them, to claim my place here. I needed a job to survive.

The parade of sky-high heels lining the room served as a stark reminder of the perilous path I was about to walk. Fully dressed once more, my heart pounding, I made my way back to where I had begun. A man in an ill-fitted suit, round-bellied with the confidence of someone who had seen it all, waited for me. His expression gave nothing away, but then, with a nod of approval, he confirmed my future. And then came the question I hadn't even allowed myself to consider: "What's your stage name?"

My mind raced, spinning at the possibilities. I'd done it. I'd been offered the job. I blurted out the first name that came to my mind—my childhood best friend: "Hannah."

"We have an Anna already. Choose again," he said, his tone flat, brooking no argument. For a moment, my mind went blank. *Choose again?* I hadn't even thought about my first choice, let alone a second. But then, without hesitation, as if the name had been waiting for me all along, I said it.

"Heather."

And in that moment, like a phoenix rising from the ashes of my former self, she was born.

It wasn't just a name but rather a shield, a role I was stepping into with both trepidation and unspoken relief. She would be armor, my protector, the version of me who could navigate this world with confidence and a carefully measured detachment.

On my first night as Heather, I wasn't sure if I was losing myself or simply discovering another version of me. In this world of smoke and mirrors, I quickly learned the unspoken rules of engagement. The club took its cut—20 percent of every chip sold—while cash exchanged hands in silent transactions, the amounts never to be disclosed. A strict code of conduct governed our interactions: Never give out personal information, always return business cards, and be sure to inform customers of your next shift. The art of seduction—and the business of it—became a finely honed skill. I quickly learned to memorize a customer's name within the first minute and charm them with wit and compliments designed to lure them from the bar to the privacy of a dance booth, where higher earning potential waited, as well as the chance of gaining their loyalty so they'd be more likely to come back and find me again during my next shift.

As I navigated my new reality, I couldn't help but draw parallels between my new profession and the world of business I had left behind. Both realms required polished performances and the ability to captivate an audience, whether in a boardroom, shop floor, or on a stage. The false identities I crafted served the same purpose: to protect my true self and maintain a semblance of control in an unpredictable world. Yet, as I would come to learn, the truth has a way of asserting itself, no matter how carefully we construct our facades. The mission to uphold these secret identities can become all-consuming, a tightrope walk between reinvention and losing one's sense of self entirely.

Between laps of the floor in revealing dresses and lining up for the next customer to walk through the door to be seated, dancers of all nationalities were called to the stage to perform their routines. The only escape from this strict rotation was to be booked in the private room. Unknowingly, I had chosen to work at one of the most exclusive, high-earning clubs in the city, where real money was made behind closed doors. As soon as your name was called, you requested your song, performed your routine, and attempted to lock eyes with as many thirsty men as possible. I can still feel their gazes today, a reminder of the power I held and the price I paid for it.

Following protocol, you waited until your replacement arrived before descending the stage, so the stage was never left empty. You then took your place on the dance podium, awaiting your next call of duty. Time on the podium was costly, reducing potential earnings from working the floor. However, it offered a sneaky way to view the club from a bird's-eye view and scan the customers until you find your next prey.

I had only one problem prior to starting: a fifty-pound entrance fee to dance, and I was broke. Not just a little broke, but no-money-to-my-name broke. The club was meant to be my way out, but I was faced with the crushing realization that I didn't know how I would get in. I'd been offered a job; I'd chosen a stage name. I was so close to making the leap into this new life, but without money, I couldn't actually begin. As my eyes readjusted to harsh daylight, I ducked into a nearby alley, desperately avoiding the curious glances of passersby. My heart raced as I fumbled for my phone and, without hesitation, dialed the one number I swore I'd never call in this situation: Mum.

The issue wasn't that she wouldn't help me out of a short-term predicament; it was that I needed a solution to a large problem that I called my life and future. I decided to keep it simple and direct: "Mum, I auditioned for a strip club and I need money to work." I could almost hear the gears turning in her mind, processing the weight of my words. Why did she ask no questions? Did she worry for the safety of her only daughter? Reflecting back now, I wonder what went through my mother's mind in that very moment. Was she deciding to let me make my own mistakes, or did she have an unwavering faith that I would be okay?

"Okay, I will send it now. Please stay safe," she said.

The line went dead. The exchange was short, almost painfully to the point. But I was back in the game. I once again made my way into the underworld, this time no longer as Jade but as Heather.

And Heather was ready for war.

As I stepped through the club's doors, I felt the weight of my past slipping away, replaced by the uncertain promise of a future I had yet to write. As my eyes adjusted to the dim lighting, I caught glimpses of the cast of characters that would become my new family—or perhaps my fiercest competitors. On my way back to the dressing room, I passed a dirty blonde with an otherworldly air about her. She was perched at the bar, long fingers wrapped around a champagne flute, deep in conversation with a silver-haired man who couldn't take his eyes off her. There was something in her serene expression that hinted at hidden depths, a mystery I found myself eager to understand.

In the shadowy corner, partially hidden by a velvet curtain the color of spilled wine, sat Viktor, one of the club's stern-faced bouncers. His massive frame seemed almost too large for the narrow space, and his unyielding scowl would become a constant presence. At first, I found him intimidating, but I would come to realize in the weeks ahead that Viktor's gruff demeanor was a shield for his surprising kindness and protectiveness as he watched over us with a vigilant eye, ready to put out any trouble before it could ignite. I owe my life to Viktor. Without him, I shudder to think about what could have happened on a fateful night, years later, when everything had gone terribly wrong.

But well before that, on my first official day, I found the dressing room to be a safe haven, with girls of all shapes and sizes, their chatter a mix of languages and accents from around the globe. Each woman, I realized, was a living, breathing novel that had a story and a reason for being here that was as complex as my own. As I sat at an empty mirror, trying desperately to make sense of how rapidly my world was shifting beneath my feet, I was jolted back to reality by a voice sharp as a stiletto heel.

A petite Eastern European glanced up from applying her bold lipstick. "You're new," she remarked, her voice carrying the crisp edge of someone who had seen many others come and go. It was a statement of fact rather than a greeting, her tone conveying an unspoken hierarchy of experience and survival. She flicked a glance at me, her eyes briefly meeting mine with a spark of curiosity before returning to her reflection. The way she moved, methodical and precise, suggested a lifetime of navigating this world with practiced ease.

Even though she hadn't asked my name, I wanted to speak it anyway, to assert my new identity and claim the name I'd chosen.

"Heather," I said, the name still feeling foreign as the word came out of my mouth shyly, as if I wasn't quite sure who Heather was yet. "I'm Heather."

To my surprise, though she'd seemed dismissive at first, she spoke again, this time slower and delivering a piece of advice that would become my mantra in this new world: "Trust no one...." Her eyes flicked briefly to meet mine before returning to her reflection. "Not even yourself." Her eyes remained glued to her reflection, her hand steady as she continued to paint her lips, the moment over as quickly as it had come.

I nodded, trying to absorb the weight of her words while adjusting the lace of my lingerie. My everyday identity soon disappeared as I donned the tools of my new trade: sheer stockings that whispered promises with every movement, and a black lace lingerie set that left little to the imagination yet somehow magnified the mystery.

She continued to apply her makeup with deliberate strokes, her gaze still fixed on the mirror. "If you're smart, you'll keep your distance from everyone," she said, her voice dropping to a conspiratorial whisper. "The club is full of people who'll pretend to be your friend, but remember, it's all part of the game. Watch who you trust and who you allow to see your true self." My new friend, or maybe my rival, looked at me, her eyes reflecting a hardness that suggested she'd learned this lesson the hard way. "You don't have to take my word for it, but you'll see soon enough."

As I embraced my new role as Heather, I couldn't help but reflect on the world beyond the club's four walls. People everywhere live with false identities and highly refined egos, each for their own complex reasons. Social pressures and societal expectations set impossibly high standards for success, beauty, and behavior, compelling individuals to present versions of themselves that align with these ideals, even if they're far removed from their authentic selves. The fear of rejection looms large, haunting those who worry their true selves won't be accepted or valued. Insecurity and low self-esteem whisper into our ears, stirring up insidious doubts, convincing many that their genuine identity isn't worthy of love or admiration. And so, like actors on a grand stage, people create personas they believe will garner the approval they so desperately crave.

I caught sight of myself in the mirror, and the woman staring back at me was both familiar and strange. Heather looked confident, alluring—a siren poised to captivate. Yet beneath the carefully applied makeup and the daring outfit, traces of Jade lingered—scared, uncertain, but fiercely determined to survive.

Armored in lace, I stopped before exiting the dressing room. Suddenly, a paralyzing realization froze me in my place: I was about to step into a world where my words and body would be my only weapons. There was no turning back; I had spent my last fifty pounds on the promise of a future I couldn't yet see. With a breath that did little to calm my racing heart, I pushed back the curtain.

I stepped onto the stage. The lights, the eyes, the challenge—welcome to the jungle, indeed.

CHAPTER 5

WELCOME TO THE JUNGLE

Like an oasis in the jungle, the club stood as a gathering place for the thirsty—not for water, but for connection, escape, and the intoxicating promise of fantasy. It was a watering hole for love-starved men and restless souls, a place where mind-numbing spirits flowed freely, temporarily quenching the parched throats of those seeking escape from the harsh realities of their lives.

As I scanned the room, I felt the weight of countless desires and motivations pressing in around me. The club floor, much like the wilds of nature, revealed the raw complexities of human behavior and primal instincts, all playing out under the seductive glow of carefully placed lights. Here, beneath the veil of civility, the same patterns of power, hunger, and hierarchy that governed the wild played out in slow, intoxicating dances.

At first glance, it might just look like another nightclub. But once inside, you begin to notice the undercurrents—the tension, the unspoken rules, the way people move with purpose and guarded intention. Internally, the club was an ecosystem in its own right. Primal instinct ran rampant, barely contained by the thin disguise of civilization. Competition hung thick in the air, as palpable as the heady mixture of perfume and cologne that mingled in the atmosphere. At the center of it all stood the stage, a shimmering mirage of possibilities and delusion. Here, dancers moved with practiced grace, their bodies both the bait and the spectacle. Each performance was a carefully choreographed seduction aimed at captivating the audience and luring in the next willing victim. Everyone came looking for something. Some for power, others for validation, and perhaps some came looking for themselves.

As I navigated this treacherous terrain, the words, "Don't trust anyone," echoed in my mind like a silent prayer. Yet, paradoxically, I found myself desperately in need of guidance, utterly lost in this unfamiliar world. The night was still young, the energy deceptively calm, but I could feel the predatory gazes of other dancers upon me. They watched with the intensity of panthers eyeing potential prey, sizing up the newcomer in their midst.

Teetering on my sky-high heels, I timidly picked up the tail of my gown, trying to avoid drawing any more attention to myself. With as much grace as I could muster, I made my way to what appeared to be a line of girls positioned next to the floor tables. Curiosity got the better of me, and I leaned toward a tall, slender brunette ahead of me in line.

"Why are we standing here?" I asked in a hushed whisper, careful not to disturb the quiet anticipation in the air.

The brunette slowly turned, her kohl-rimmed eyes appraising me with a mixture of amusement and pity. "First night?" she asked. A knowing smirk appeared on her scarlet lips as if she had witnessed this scene play out countless times before. "We're waiting for the customers to show up," she explained. "It's all about positioning, darling. You want to be in the right place when the money comes through that door."

I always thought meeting a man at the club was like rolling dice, a blend of timing and luck. I was unaware then how little luck played into it. It wasn't until later, with the help of my new-found ally Rose—the very same brunette—that I uncovered the truth. The seating of clients was anything but random. The club was more than just dancers and customers; behind the scenes were many players, each with their own role in this high-stakes game. It was a carefully coordinated affair, managed by discreet tips handed to the doormen who acted as gatekeepers and strategically seated each visitor around the club. When three clients were seated, the next three girls in line had a chance to connect. If a customer turned out to be uninterested or a dud, you either returned to the line or took a calculated risk by prowling the floor for a more prom-ising suitor.

"If you want to make real money, babe, you have to work smarter, not harder."

And just like that, Rose let me in on the first real secret of the club—connections were currency. As I was enlightened on the internal tipping system, I realized I had stumbled into a business far more complex than I had ever imagined. Building relation-ships was a survival tactic, helping you get better clients and pro-tect yourself. First, there were the doormen; they were crucial allies in this game of chance and strategy. Their power to lead new customers to specific tables made them invaluable assets. You wanted them in your corner…literally. Then came the chip girls, a savvy bunch who could be bribed for insider informa-tion. They handled the transactions and knew who was just there to look and who was willing to spend thousands. A heavy metal card in a customer's hand was like gold, and negotiating a percentage of your backroom earnings with these girls could mean the difference between a lucrative night and going home empty-handed.

The bartenders, silent observers of the nightly dance of seduction, were not to be overlooked. Their sympathetic ears often caught the desperate whispers of dancers struggling to turn a profit. Cultivating their goodwill could result in shots of water masquerading as vodka—a clever tactic for encouraging "ANOTHER ROUND!" while keeping your wits about you as you skillfully drain your client's pockets.

The DJ controlled the rhythm of the night, and a discreetly placed twenty-pound bill could make your name disappear from the rotation, granting you extra time with a potentially lucrative client. It sounds small, but controlling the music meant controlling the spotlight, and with it, your chances of closing a deal. Knowing how to influence these hidden controls gave some dancers a big advantage. But towering above them all in importance was the duty manager—the gatekeeper to your big earnings. In the hazy early hours of each morning, as the club began to run dry and the incessant beat of the speakers left you feeling drunk and disassociated, it was his stamp of approval you needed to secure your night's work. Winning him over wasn't just advantageous; it was essential.

As I absorbed this wealth of information, my head spinning with the intricacies of club politics, I realized that recruiting your tribe was not for the faint of heart. Like any social group, you had to figure out who was on your side and who wasn't. Building your circle was as much about protecting yourself as it was about business. The alliances you made could mean the difference between thriving or fading away. The meticulous strategy required to succeed was just another piece of the highly refined skill set that would keep wealthy clients coming back week after week. You could be a great dancer, but if you didn't understand how to work the politics and navigate the relationships, you would not succeed in this environment of enemies and allies.

But on that first night, standing in line with Rose, I knew nothing of this world. I was a novice, desperately in need of a crash course that would help me figure out how this all worked. Suddenly, the heavy wooden doors swung open with a resounding thud. Two young men in impeccably tailored suits were escorted to our side of the floor by the doorman. They carried themselves with an ease that suggested they were used to being in rooms like this. I watched, wide-eyed, as Rose sprang into action, her movements fluid and purposeful as she draped her lithe body across one man's lap when he was seated.

Frantically, I tried to mimic her every move, awkwardly perching myself on the other man's knee. Rose, sensing my nervousness, smoothly signaled the waitress to bring over drinks. Her intention was clear—to loosen up the guys, and me by extension, as her success also depended on my performance. As the drinks arrived, I found myself caught between two very different men. There was Tom, resplendent in his Savile Row suit, his laughter echoing hollowly in the charged atmosphere. Beside him sat James, his Rolex gleaming as brightly as his grand gestures and overstuffed wallet. James, I would later learn, would become a regular of mine, and then some, but for now, he remained reserved, more observer than participant in the unfolding drama. This was a subtle power play, a test of who controlled the room and who watched from the sidelines. I didn't realize it yet, but I was assessing him just as closely, learning to read the signs—who to engage and who to watch carefully.

"No dances for me tonight, ladies," James declared, his voice tinged with a hint of something deliberate, something that felt like a challenge.

Rose, undeterred, flashed a dazzling smile. "Oh, come on," she purred, her voice laced with playful insistence. "We can all go together."

James let that moment stretch, looking directly into what felt like my soul. Then, with an effortless flick of his wrist, he slipped a crisp note into my hand. "Here, take this and show Tom a good time."

Before I could process what was happening, Rose's fingers were wrapping around my wrist, hoisting both Tom and me toward the public dancing quarters. My stomach clenched with a mixture of excitement and terror as we approached the tiered rows of brightly lit booths overlooking the main stage.

As we settled into a booth, the vulnerability of our exposed position struck me. These booths were designed to hide very little from prying eyes. This exposure wasn't accidental—it was part of the psychological game, heightening tension and excitement for both dancers and clients, making every glance and gesture charged with meaning. And that, as I was about to discover, was precisely the point. Rose moved with the sinuous grace of a snake, her body undulating to the beat as she slowly, teasingly, began to remove her dress. Her eyes never left Tom's face, the intensity of her gaze a masterclass in the art of magnetism.

Taking my cue from Rose, I positioned myself with one leg on the ground and the other knee on the couch, bringing myself tantalizingly close to Tom. I could feel his hot breath on my neck, our bodies mere inches apart, the air between us crackling with tension. I glanced at James across the room, still seated at the table, observing. There was something in the way he held his drink, something in the way he didn't look away.

My standing leg threatened to buckle beneath me as Rose's performance reached its climax, her underwear falling away to reveal her statuesque form in nothing but stockings and heels. The ticking of an invisible clock seemed to grow louder in my ears—this would be my only crash course tonight, I realized. I tried to absorb everything I could from Rose's performance, after which I knew I'd be on my own. One dance, one song, one chance to learn the ropes for the long night ahead. As I prepared myself for what was next, my heart raced with anticipation. This was my initiation into the path I had either chosen or was predestined for me, and from this moment on, everything would change.

Oh, how naive I was to think I could take in all I needed from that single dance. As the melody shifted to something more sultry, I stumbled upon another crucial tactic in this intricate dance of desire: upselling. The art, I quickly learned, was in the timing—waiting until the very last seconds to remove that final layer, offering just a glimpse. This wasn't just about teasing, it was a calculated move, designed to leave the customer hungry for more.

"Do you want us to keep going?" Rose's voice dripped with feigned innocence as she glanced over her shoulder, her body bent provocatively over the banister. The question hung in the air, laden with promise. But she didn't wait for an answer. She had already begun to move her hips in a hypnotic rhythm and then threaded her fingers through Tom's hair with an intimacy so practiced it could almost be mistaken for real.

In that moment, something shifted within me. With a boldness I didn't know I possessed, I reached down and scooped up Tom's wallet from the couch. Our eyes met, and I gave him a look that brooked no argument, one where I held all the power. Who was this Heather? And where had she found this sudden fire?

The rush was intoxicating. In less than fifteen minutes, I had earned one hundred and twenty pounds. Another trick of the trade revealed itself: Always ask for a tip at the end, a gesture of gratitude for services rendered. We returned Tom to James, slightly disheveled but grinning like a man who had no regret. Rose, never one to let an opportunity slip away, made one last attempt to entice James. His eyes raked over Tom's partially unbuttoned shirt, looking just a second too long before he shook his head with a polite decline.

As we prepared to move on, I said my goodbyes and retrieved my drink. Yet, as I turned to leave, a peculiar sensation settled in the pit of my stomach, a premonition telling me that this wouldn't be the last time our paths would cross with these two men. And fate, as it turned out, had no intention of proving me wrong.

I hadn't been left to fend for myself after our time with Tom. Rose and I formed a double act and became allies that night. Our contrasting physiques—her slender body, a counterpoint to my petite yet curvy frame—made us a formidable team. Together, we could dominate a solitary soul or entertain a group with equal ease. The night unfolded relatively tamely, and by 2 a.m., I was 340 pounds richer. My pockets were heavier, my nerves steadier, and my sense of self irrevocably altered.

With the wad of notes gripped tightly in my hand, buried deep within the folds of my coat pocket, I ran through the deserted streets back to my basement room on Drummond Street—the only place that still felt like mine. The moment my head hit the pillow it was as if my spirit came back into my body. I was Jade again, and it almost felt as though the night and Heather had never happened.

Except it did happen, and not only would it happen again, but it was about to become a lot riskier.

CHAPTER 6

THE TRUTH IN OUR SCARS

The glitter dusted on my skin caught the light, a shimmering reminder of the illusion I had created—the persona the world saw when they looked at me, a carefully worn mask that both hid and protected the real me underneath. In the space between what is and what could be, we face both our deepest fears and our greatest potential. Everything involves risk, including not doing anything; even staying still can have consequences we don't see right away. As I adjusted my lingerie in the dressing room mirror, I pondered this truth. The quick payoff to this work, with money pressed into my palm by eager hands, showed me the potential I was just starting to tap into. But wasn't I taking a risk too? Stepping onto that stage night after night, revealing and concealing in equal measure, I gave myself over to the possibilities of the night, which I could try to direct and manipulate but ultimately could not control.

True growth often lies just beyond our comfort zones and the limited boundaries we've drawn for ourselves. I thought of my life before the club and the mundane, predictable trajectory I'd been on: university, a mediocre job, a somewhat conventional life. But here, in this world of shadows and seduction, I was discovering a world and parts of myself I never knew existed.

To take a chance is to embrace the unknown and step into the void with nothing but faith. Each time I emerged from behind the velvet curtain, I was doing just that. Yes, there were moments of doubt, wondering if I'd made the right choice. The judgmental looks from passersby on the street as I entered the club, the lies I told my friends about my new "bartending job," the lingering fear of what it all meant for my future. But it was in these hard decisions that I began to discover the depth of my own strength.

True strength is understanding that vulnerability is not a weakness, but a crucial part of the journey toward meeting the depths of your soul. Letting down your guard doesn't mean losing control; it means trusting yourself. When you dare to believe in something greater, you allow the universe to work in your favor, guiding you back to your heart and toward your destiny. Overcoming these fears is how we find our true selves hidden in our shielded hearts. For in the end, we regret not the risks we took, but the ones we didn't have the courage to take.

This isn't to say that all brave decisions turn out well. There is a dark side to risk. You may unwittingly be jumping into something that will bring untold amounts of pain. Pain that lingers, reshapes you in ways you never asked for, and leaves scars where dreams once lived. You may find yourself lost, questioning whether the leap was foolish rather than fearless. Sometimes, the cost of risk is more than you ever imagined. The truth is, not every risk leads to something better. Sometimes, it leads to heartbreak so raw it makes you wish you had never tried at all. Sometimes, it leaves you standing in the wreckage of a choice you can't take back, wondering if you mistook recklessness for courage.

But even in the depths of regret there is something to be found. Pain, though merciless, is also a teacher. It strips away illusion, forces you to face yourself, and in time, reveals a strength you didn't know you had. The dark side of risk is that it does not promise reward, only transformation.

You may fall, you may break, and you may curse the moment you dared. But safety was never the point. Growth, truth, and the unshakable knowing that you tried is what makes the risk worth taking.

In the end, it's not the pain that defines us, but what we choose to do with it.

When I woke up after the first night of the club, I lay in bed for a while, my mind still racing from the night before, the ceiling a blank canvas for my swirling thoughts. The realization of what awaited me tonight when I went back for the second time flooded my mind with questions and doubts. I had lucked out when Rose took me under her wing, but I couldn't count on that every night. If I was going to be a player in this game, I needed to up my ante. With six hours until my evening shift, I found myself wandering the streets of Soho, stepping into one shop, then another, hunting for more pieces of Heather in the elements of my new work uniform.

Heather was different from the other girls; a fact I clung to like a lifeline. My innocence had been my unexpected upper hand on that first night, and I was determined to play to my strengths. I was very aware as I worked side by side with Rose that I not only felt out of place but looked it too—a quality that, I couldn't help but notice, seemed to intrigue the men. Their eyes followed me with a fascination and desire to know more.

Trying to picture what Heather would wear, I selected a blush pink lingerie set and a red floor-length gown from the sex store hidden on the lower ground of a dilapidated tattoo studio. Not only had I felt out of place in the club the previous night, I even felt like an impostor as I made my purchase. But I reminded myself that, with these clothes, I was securing my new persona and making her more real. I amped myself up for another night on the pole.

Nikki, the house mother I'd met at my audition, raised an eyebrow as I arrived early. Her eyes told a story of years of experience beyond this world, holding a mix of surprise and something else as she looked me up and down. A silent question hung between us. Was it concern or curiosity? I brushed it off. I didn't have the time to try to figure it out. I had work to do and money to make. I was determined to get a better sense of the lay of the land before the night commenced. Already, seasoned pros were perched at the bar, entertaining men who'd clearly come straight from their corporate cages. Maybe nobody was going to give me a rule book, but I had my own superpower: my ability to pay attention. I absorbed every detail, every unspoken rule. The afternoon shift, I learned, was a different beast altogether—fewer men, but the potential of striking gold if you played your cards right. Experience was the currency here, and patience was the key to spending it well.

The rules revealed themselves to me slowly through experience and observation. Starting the night early meant paying the lowest fee to dance, but arriving later, you had to pay more. The beginning of the evening was painfully slow, which frustrated me and made me wonder if I should cut my losses and start my shift later for my mental sanity. However, I soon realized this calm before the storm was invaluable. These quiet hours were my training ground. The club wasn't as crazy yet, and more space was available for me to hone my craft and practice the subtle art of seduction. During these earlier hours, I built relationships with returning clients, listening to their stories of deep unhappiness at their jobs, with their bosses, with their wives, and their dreams of a future that would probably never materialize. Although part of me knew these conversations were often a waste of potential earnings, they brought me a strange comfort and grounded me. In the lull before the chaos, I felt my new persona coming to life.

The energy on Friday night was frenetic, the kind of night where anything could happen. Twice as many dancers jostled for attention, and the crowd was thicker, wilder, unpredictable. From corporate sharks to rowdy bachelor parties, landing the best possible customer was a game of chance with sky-high stakes. The convergence of laughter, shouts, and music blended into a singular, pulsating beat that seemed to drive the night forward.

Twenty pounds was the lowest someone could pay for a dance, but I quickly learned that the potential for earnings was limitless. It was during my first weekend that I caught my first glimpse of the infamous backroom. As I signed the covenant "What happens in the backroom, stays in the backroom," I had to wonder what secrets lay behind that curtain.

Every night was a delicate balance of holding control and letting things flow. Fortunes could be earned in a heartbeat but they were not guaranteed. The only certainty was the promise of the unexpected, and that raw sense of potential that may or may not come to fruition. As I scanned the crowd as I waited for my turn to dance on stage, a face caught my attention. He was devastatingly handsome, with an ambiguous aura that set him apart from the drunken masses that surrounded the main stage. His tailored suit and confident demeanor suggested wealth, but there was something else, something mysterious lurking beneath his polished exterior that enticed me.

I sensed his gaze lingering on me as I moved across the stage. His intensity unnerved me, and for a few seconds, I was determined to keep my distance from him—but curiosity won over caution. He was looking for something—or someone—and maybe that someone could be me. As I walked across the stage with deliberate steps, a quiet voice inside me warned against him, instinct whispering caution, but a newfound recklessness took over. I met his eyes as I gripped the pole, dropping to my knees in a move that was part defiance, part invitation.

I finished my solo show and exited the stage, my heart racing from the performance and the intense gaze I'd felt throughout. As I stepped onto the main floor, I began to prowl through the crowd, my movements deliberate and sensual like a predator in stilettos—equal parts hunter and hunted. I was acutely aware of his presence, though I feigned nonchalance, acting busy and unbothered, like I had better things to do than pay attention to him. But there was no denying the spark that had ignited between us. Something about his energy had already intertwined with mine from that single, smoldering look we'd shared.

I could feel his eyes tracking my every move, but I pretended to be engrossed in the atmosphere of clinking glasses, laughter, and the seductive hum of conversation, all the while hyperaware of where he sat in the shadows. Suddenly, I felt a tap on my shoulder. I turned, half-expecting–half-hoping to see him standing there. Instead, I was met with the knowing smirk of one of the chip girls. "You've been requested for a dance," she said. There was a glint in her eye that told me this was no ordinary request.

My eyes wandered through the crowd, a deliberate scan that concealed the rising excitement within me. Suddenly, as if drawn by a hidden force, they locked with his. He was in the same secluded corner, shrouded in shadows that seemed to promise sinfully forbidden pleasures. At that moment, the rest of the room faded into the background, leaving only the magnetic pull between us. With a deliberate slowness, he raised his drink, signaling me to come. It was an invitation, a challenge, and a promise all rolled into one.

As I began to make my way toward him, weaving through the crowd with practiced ease, I couldn't shake the feeling that I was walking toward something that I had never yet experienced before. Who was this mysterious man? What did he want? And more importantly, was I ready for whatever game he was about to play?

"You called?" I purred, stepping into his orbit with a confidence that felt rehearsed yet strangely real. Under the facade of Heather, my heart pounded, a steady reminder that Jade was very much present despite my best efforts to hide her.

"Impressive show you put on," he said smoothly.

"First time here?" I asked, feigning nonchalance as I crossed my legs, the deliberate movement parting my dress just enough to tease. The game had begun.

He studied me, his expression unreadable. "Something like that," he replied. "I'm here on business."

I tilted my head, intrigued. "And what kind of business is that?"

He finished his drink, his fingers tapping idly against the glass, but his eyes never leaving mine. "The kind that pays well if you know what you're doing."

Emboldened by experience, by the countless nights of practice, I leaned in. "Well, why don't we go for a dance so you can see what I can do?"

He didn't answer immediately. Instead, he lifted a finger, summoning the waitress with an effortless command.

"Cristal," he ordered, his intent clear. "For the backroom."

A palpable tension lingered between us, an indication that secrets were about to be uncovered. Every silent exchange between us carried the weight of anticipation, as if the universe itself was conspiring to bring our hidden truths into the light.

As we navigated our way through the writhing crowd, I felt the club's essence pressing in on us. This was a place where secrets and truth intertwined like lovers, where appearances were as deceptive as they were revealing. Here, nothing was ever quite what it seemed. Every glance, every touch, every whispered word could hold a double meaning. In this shadowy realm, instincts weren't just useful, they were essential. On the exterior, my new customer exuded confidence, success, and control—a man accustomed to getting exactly what he wanted. And of course, I played my part too: the seductive dancer, mysterious and untouchable. I watched his hands as they pushed back the curtain, strong and sure, and wondered about the duality they held. Were they hands that built or destroyed? That reached for things only to let them go?

We eased into the plush seating, settling into the private world as he poured the champagne. As I accepted the glass, our fingers brushed, and for a moment, I thought I saw a flicker of vulnerability in his eyes. It vanished so quickly I wondered if I'd imagined it.

"To new acquaintances," he murmured, his voice low and inviting.

I raised my glass, meeting his gaze. "And to the stories we tell ourselves."

He arched an eyebrow, intrigued. "And what story do you tell yourself, I wonder?"

I took a slow sip of champagne, buying time, considering my response. In this moment, it was as if my soul spoke a revelation to me: What would life look like if people were to know the truth? If we stripped away the artifice, the carefully constructed narratives we present to the world, what would remain? It struck me then how much of what we show the world is carefully crafted—a mask or story we tell to protect ourselves or to fit in. We all have these layers, stories that help us make sense of who we are and how we want others to see us. But sometimes, these stories can become so fixed, they keep us from being truly known or connecting deeply.

As I wondered whether I should deflect or answer his question, I thought about how hard I'd worked to bring Heather to life, to make her untouchable. Was I going to strip her away, just because he'd asked? Show him the true me that lived underneath? What truth did I owe not this man, but myself?

"That depends," I finally answered, swirling the golden liquid in my glass. "Are you asking about Heather's story…or mine?"

We all tell stories about who we are, building versions of ourselves we think others want to hear or see on social media. Sometimes, these stories protect us. Other times, they keep us from truly connecting. We yearn for authenticity while fearing exposure. My question begs whether these portrayals act as shields, safeguarding our vulnerable cores, or prisons limiting our potential for genuine belonging. Do we lose touch with our authentic selves in the process, becoming actors in a play we've scripted but no longer understand? And how can we reconnect who we truly are to be fully seen?

If we were to peel back the layers of pretense and expose our raw, unvarnished selves to the harsh light of day, what tableau would unfold before us? We might witness a paradigm shift in human relations, or perhaps we'd stand naked in our vulnerabilities, our hidden desires, our unspoken fears, feeling a new sense of freedom in the choice to expose ourselves. The social hierarchies built on perceived perfection might collapse, giving way to a more egalitarian way of relating and catalyzing a collective journey toward self-actualization. In stripping away the artifice, we might find that truth itself is multifaceted, that our essence is not a fixed point but a constantly evolving spectrum. Perhaps the most profound revelation would be that authenticity is not about adhering to a single, immutable self, but about embracing the complex, sometimes contradictory nature of our being.

Ultimately, a world in which we speak the absolute truth about ourselves might challenge us to redefine concepts of identity, relationships, and social harmony. It would compel us to confront the beauty and terror of our naked selves, and in doing so, perhaps unlock new frontiers of human potential and connection. That night, I felt the potential of my choice. If I answered truthfully, what might be unlocked? On the other hand, what would I be risking?

Setting down his glass, he leaned in close, his lips nearly brushing my ear. "Why don't you show me?" he whispered, his words both a temptation and a challenge. His hand found my waist, pulling me closer, and the heat of his touch seeped through the thin fabric of my dress. As we sat there, the boundary between professional facade and personal desire became blurred.

"You know," he murmured, his eyes following the curve of my hip, "I think we're all searching for something real, even in places like this. A connection that goes beyond the surface, beyond the fantasy." With practiced grace, I reached for the clasp of my top.

"Maybe we can find a bit of truth together," I said, my voice low and inviting. "Would you like that?"

He nodded, almost imperceptibly.

Slowly, I began to remove my clothes. Unlike my previous times stripping in this very club, tonight, each piece of clothing felt weighted with meaning. As I undressed, I felt like I was stripping away pieces of Heather, of the persona I'd built. As I danced for him, I let a bit of my true self shine through—the woman beneath the seductress.

What followed wasn't just a transaction but a dance of intimacy unlike anything I'd experienced before, as I slowly peeled back the layer of pretense to reveal the raw, beautiful essence beneath. As the night deepened, so did our connection. We shared stories, fears, and dreams. I'd spent my childhood protecting myself against pain, always holding a shield toward the world. But in this hidden corner of the world, on this night, I lowered my defenses. We found a freedom neither of us had known before—the freedom to be utterly, unashamedly ourselves. The club seemed to shine a light on our shared desire for liberation from life as we both knew it, inviting us to explore the depths of authenticity beneath the surface of social expectations and my pink lingerie.

As the city started slowly awakening, and the significance of this connection sat heavily in my purse. I found myself reflecting on the question that had unraveled the evening and the spark that inspired such an unexpected turn of events. *And what story do you tell yourself, I wonder?* What would be the story I told myself now? I was two thousand pounds richer, but the money felt almost incidental compared to what had transpired. In the dim light of the private booth, two strangers had managed to find a moment of genuine connection—something I never thought possible in a place like this.

Come Sunday, my body ached from the previous night's exertions, feet blistered from hours in impossibly high heels, but a quiet satisfaction lingered beneath the exhaustion. The memory of my retail job, once a source of monotonous stability, now felt like a relic from another life. In a single night, I had earned more than I'd made in an entire month of folding sweaters, running credit cards, and plastering on fake smiles for disgruntled customers. Names might blur and faces fade, but the possibility of more nights like the one I'd just had was intoxicating to me. I'd learned something valuable: Sometimes, the bravest thing you can do is let someone see a glimpse of your true self. It's risky, especially in a place built on delusion, but the payoff can be extraordinary. That connection, even if it's just for a moment, can be exactly what both people need.

I knew not every night would be like this one. There'd still be the usual parade of drunk businessmen, rowdy bachelor parties, and guys just looking for a thrill. But now I saw the potential for more. Each interaction was a chance to connect, to understand, to see and be seen, even if only for the length of a song.

I wonder when you last allowed someone to see your true self. This, I believe, is the greatest act of courage. When we take that leap, there might be pain or rejection waiting—but we also might just find the connection we've been searching for all along. Some might be fleeting, a reason to learn or grow in a specific moment. Other connections could last a season, accompanying you through a chapter of life. And perhaps, just perhaps, one might stretch into a lifetime.

CHAPTER 7

ASK NO QUESTIONS, HEAR NO LIES

In the dancing booths, my conversations were often stripped of pretense. Lonely businessmen nursing their drinks, blushing bachelors nervously fumbling their words, even women exploring their desires. Each sought a fleeting moment of connection in this realm of fantasy.

It was a strange paradox of being free to become whoever I wanted to be, yet somehow feeling more myself than ever. Each night, as I decided what outfit I would adorn my body in, I also decided what story I would tell that night. There was a crafty art in quickly understanding what a customer wanted and what fantasy would fill your purse. I had already noticed that men were drawn to me for my innocence, and soon realized it was because they loved to play the role of the savior. And the cruelest irony? Deep down, I wanted to be saved too. The fantasy I enacted might have been to please the man, but also, in its own twisted way, it was comforting to the little girl in me who wanted someone to come along and make everything okay. Perhaps that was the greatest illusion of all, the idea that salvation could ever come from anyone but myself.

One night, a man whose presence felt heavier than the usual crowd walked in. His eyes were a deep brown that mirrored my own but carried a sadness deeper than loneliness. He introduced himself as Paul, a widower in his early forties. As I led him to a private booth, I could feel his grief hanging between us like a tangible thing.

He looked at me—really looked at me—in a way that made me feel both seen and exposed.

"What brings you here tonight, Paul?" I asked lightly.

"I'm not sure," he admitted. "I…I guess I'm trying to remember what it feels like to be alive."

In that moment, I made a decision. Tonight, I wouldn't be the seductress or the innocent ingenue. Tonight, I would be a confidant, a listener, a temporary balm for a wounded soul desperate for relief. As I listened to him speak of his small steps toward healing, I felt a strange ache in my chest. Here was a man who had faced unimaginable loss, yet he was actively working toward his own salvation. And what was I doing? Hiding behind different personas, waiting for someone to come along and give my life meaning. Hours passed, and we barely noticed. When it was time for him to leave, he took my hand and pressed a generous tip into it. "Thank you," he said, his voice thick with emotion.

As I watched him walk away, I felt a strange mix of elation and emptiness. Maybe I had made a real difference in someone's life tonight, perhaps even helped him take a step toward healing. But as the club's neon lights flickered off and dawn began to break, I couldn't shake the feeling that I was still waiting for my own savior.

The next few weeks brought a parade of familiar faces and new clients, each with their own stories and desires. There was Jake, the young tech entrepreneur who came in buzzing with excitement over his first big sale. His bravado masked a nervous insecurity I could almost feel beneath his confident act. I played the role of the adoring fan, feeding his need to be king of his world.

Then there was Melissa, a woman in her thirties who came in with a group of friends for a bachelorette party. At first, she danced and laughed like the rest, but as the night wore on, Melissa's mask slipped. She confessed her terror of commitment and envy of her friends' certainty about marriage.

I held space for her fears, reminding her that vulnerability is not weakness but courage. As I listened to her, I felt a deep resonance within myself. I had my own fear of commitment, rooted in the pain of my father's abandonment. I understood all too well the paralyzing fear of being hurt, of opening yourself up only to be left behind. It was a struggle I grappled with daily and a constant internal battle between longing for connection and wanting to protect myself from potential pain. In comforting Melissa, I found myself speaking to my own wounded heart, reminding us both that while the risk of hurt is real, so too is the possibility of love and genuine connection. It was a bittersweet moment of recognition between two women in this unexpected place.

That night, after my shift ended, I sat in front of my vanity mirror. As I slowly removed the glitter, false lashes, and layers of makeup, I stared at my reflection. I hadn't truly seen this face in months. The harsh fluorescent light above me seemed to strip away more than just cosmetics.

"What's your story?" I asked the girl in the mirror. "What do you really want?"

The answer came to me in a sudden, crystal-clear moment of clarity. I wanted to write. Not just dream about it, not just scribble in journals between shifts, but really write. To tell stories that mattered, that touched people's lives the way my conversations in the club did, but on a grander scale. The fantasy of being saved had its allure, its comfort. Maybe there would always be a piece of me that longed for that. But I was starting to realize that waiting for a savior was not going to serve me. That true salvation, true fulfillment, could only come from within. I might not have all the answers, might still struggle with the desire for someone to swoop in and make everything better. But for now, for today, I was allowing myself to hold on to a dream. This wasn't the final step, but the first. And that, I realized, was how you start to save yourself.

Wanting to be saved—by someone or something—is something many of us carry deep inside. Often, it comes from wounds we picked up as children and stories our culture tells us about needing rescue. This desire can manifest in various ways throughout our lives, influencing not only our relationships but also our decision-making processes and overall well-being. Understanding this phenomenon requires a multifaceted approach, blending psychological research with spiritual insights and the raw truth of lived experiences.

Research has shown that individuals with anxious attachment styles are more likely to idealize romantic partners and seek excessive reassurance, essentially looking for someone to "save" them from their own insecurities. This pattern can persist into adulthood, manifesting as a search for a romantic partner, mentor, or even a spiritual figure who can provide the unconditional love and security that may have been lacking in childhood.

The concept of the "inner child" in psychology suggests that unresolved childhood wounds continue to influence adult behavior. The part of us that yearns to be saved often represents this wounded inner child, seeking the love, protection, and validation that may have been missing during crucial developmental stages—and I know this from my own experience. When those needs go unmet, they don't simply disappear; they find new ways to express themselves. Sometimes, they emerge as unhealthy relationship patterns. Other times, they show up in self-sabotage, impostor syndrome, or an inability to fully trust ourselves. Beyond the psychological, there is a physiological element to this as well. Trauma, especially in childhood, can disrupt the normal development of self-soothing mechanisms, leaving us to seek external sources of comfort and safety. The nervous system, conditioned by past experiences, can mistake intensity for connection, instability for passion, and control for safety. This neurobiological impact can reinforce the psychological desire to be rescued or saved by someone else. But the truth, the terrifying, liberating truth, is that no one is coming to save us.

Beyond psychology, many spiritual traditions address the human longing for salvation or enlightenment, offering various paths to transcendence or union with the divine. In Christianity, the concept of salvation through Christ speaks directly to this desire. The idea that one can be rescued from sin and granted eternal life through faith taps into deep-seated human longings for redemption and unconditional love. It provides a sense of safety, a reassurance that no matter how lost we feel, there is always a way home.

Buddhist philosophy, while not framed in terms of being "saved" by an external force, offers a path to liberation from suffering through enlightenment and self-awareness. In many New Age spiritual movements, the concept of "healing the inner child" has gained prominence. These practices often blend psychological insights with spiritual techniques, encouraging individuals to connect with and nurture their wounded inner selves through meditation, visualization, and energy work.

Recognizing that the desire to be saved isn't just mine, but something many people carry, was a turning point. Rather than chasing the idea of someone else swooping in to fix me, I began to understand what many therapists and spiritual teachers mean about self-empowerment. Healing, I realized, might not come from one grand moment, but from a mix of psychological work, spiritual practice, and honest self-reflection. For me, that meant tending to the wounded inner child, learning self-compassion, and slowly building a sense of my own strength. It's the shift from looking outward for rescue to trusting the wisdom within that can turn dependence into real independence and even healthy interdependence. This journey reflects both psychological maturation and spiritual growth, offering a holistic approach to addressing one of humanity's most profound and persistent desires. Back in those first weeks at the club, though, I was only just brushing the surface of these ideas, still figuring out what my own need to be saved really meant—and what I was going to do about it.

As the weeks passed, I found myself increasingly drawn into the stories of the strangers I encountered. Between shifts at the club, I would reflect on these lives, each story a poignant reminder of how deeply interconnected we are as humans. Each conversation revealed how our experiences, emotions, and desires are intricately linked, shedding light on the profound ways we influence and shape one another. It became evident that the mystery of existence, the complexity of human behavior, and the whispers of the spiritual realm were all converging, waiting to be explored, one word, one dance, one soul at a time.

Over time, the club started to feel like my second home. As I grew more comfortable in my role, I began to better understand the intricate web of relationships and stories that surrounded me. It was during the earlier day shifts, which had become a favorite of mine due to the lack of fierce competition and girl-eat-girl rivalry that filled the room each night, that I started to get to know each woman's story as they shared how and why they had started work in the club, and what their plan and dreams were for the future.

I was beyond inspired, and still am, by the grit and determination of those girls. They had every step figured out while I was just trying to get by, making things up as I went along. Many of them had come to London from different countries and had varying degrees of fluency in English. But the language barrier didn't seem to matter, because we spoke a deeper common language: that of emotional pain turned into power.

The irony was, as I got to know people beyond the makeup and wigs, we didn't even know each other's real names. But in a strange way, it didn't seem to matter, because who we were went so far beyond names.

There was Destiny, a single mother of two who danced to put herself through the nursing school at the hospital right next door to the club on Warren Street. Her eyes would light up when she talked about her kids, but I could see the toll the late nights took on her. "Sometimes I feel like I'm living two completely separate lives," she confided in me one night as we touched up our eyeliner in the dressing room mirror. "But I keep reminding myself it's all for them, you know?" And that was enough to keep her going. Then there was Crystal and her sister Diamond, who had moved to London for one singular purpose: to make as much money as they could to set them up for a comfortable life back in Eastern Europe. They told me how much they were working toward buying their dream house. They were disciplined, strategic, and fiercely loyal to one another. Each night, before we left, I would trade out my larger fifty-pound notes for their smaller bills so they could smuggle them back to their family in their native country.

As the nights wore on, I found myself becoming the keeper of secrets, a confidant for many of the women around. In the dressing room, between sets, stories would pour out—tales of abusive relationships, dreams deferred, and the constant struggle to maintain dignity in a world that often saw us as objects rather than people.

One particularly busy night, I noticed Chloe, one of our veteran dancers, sitting alone in the corner, her usual vibrant energy noticeably dimmed. I approached her cautiously, sensing something was off.

"Hey," I said softly, sliding onto the bench beside her. "Tough night?"

Chloe looked up, her carefully applied mascara smudged from tears she'd tried to hide. "I don't know anymore," she murmured. And just like that, another story was about to unfold.

"I saw my ex-husband out there," she whispered. "With his new wife. God, I used to be her, you know? Young, naive, thinking I was in love with a man who really saw me."

I listened as Chloe poured out her story—how she'd married young, how her husband had gradually isolated her from friends and family, how dancing had started as her way to regain some financial independence, but the independence came at a cost and ultimately led to the collapse of her marriage.

"And now here I am, thirty-five years old, still taking my clothes off for strangers while he parades around with his trophy wife," she laughed bitterly, but there was no humor in it.

I took her hand, warm and trembling, squeezing it gently as if to transfer strength through the simple touch. "You're so much more than what he reduced you to," I told her. "You're strong, you're resilient, and you're building a life on your own terms, not his."

As I spoke the words, I realized I was talking to myself as much as to Chloe—two women who had been broken down but refused to stay that way. Each night in the club chipped away at me, wearing away my innocence, while simultaneously empowering a fiercer part of me. The dichotomy was maddening at times.

There were good nights too—nights filled with laughter and a sense of camaraderie and sisterhood that I'd never experienced before. We celebrated each other's victories—Diamond finally having enough to buy her first home, Destiny passing her final exams, and Carla opening her own photography gallery in East London, which was partially funded by a generous customer from New York who took a liking to her and wanted to be a part of her success. Those moments reminded me that, despite the darkness, there was still light.

But as weeks turned into months, I noticed changes in myself. I became hyperaware of men's gazes even outside the club. It was as if I could hear their thoughts, dissecting their stares, questioning their intentions. I found it harder to form genuine connections, always wondering if people saw me as a person or a fantasy. Could I ever be just a woman again, or was I forever marked by this world? The thoughts in my mind became darker, engulfed with memories of less-than-desirable encounters as I struggled to find authenticity in a world of illusions.

As much as I valued the rewards of my leap of faith, not only in terms of material stability, but the powerful connections I'd been lucky enough to form, there was another, darker side to my life in the club. The trauma of the job was undeniable. I began to notice how many of us developed coping mechanisms—some turned to alcohol or drugs, others dissociated during dances, and some, like me, created elaborate fantasies and personas to separate our true selves from our stage identities. But these coping mechanisms, while providing temporary relief, were merely band-aids on a much deeper wound. The trauma we experienced night after night was slowly but surely leaving its mark, not just on our psyches, but on our very bodies.

I remember the night I first truly understood the price of this world. It was a particularly rough shift, and the room reeked of cheap beer and desperation. I hadn't yet even made back the money I had paid at the door to dance. As I scanned the dimly lit room, my eyes fell upon a particularly rowdy group of very drunk men. They might as well have had a flashing neon sign over their heads that screamed AVOID AT ALL COSTS. But desperation has a way of clouding judgment, and my ego got the better of me. I decided that something was better than nothing. With a practiced sway of my hips, I approached the group.

"Come with me," I purred to one of them, promising it would be worth his while.

As we entered the private dance room, I skipped my usual flirty chat and seduction, eager to get it over with, to make my money and move on. But as I began my normal act, a strange, oppressive energy seemed to fill the room. Slowly, I started to reveal my body, but the energy between us grew thicker, more sinister. An uncomfortable feeling clawed its way up my spine. Instinctively, my body tensed.

He wasn't saying anything, but there was a look in his eye that told me something was terribly wrong. It wasn't just his predatory gaze—I was somewhat used to that—but something darker within it. As he watched, his gaze seemed to strip away not just my clothes, but my very humanity. Maybe my fear was primordial, some inner guidance system built to protect us from danger, like prey might have in the animal kingdom. Whatever it was, it screamed at me to run. But before I had any chance to make sense of what was about to happen, it was already too late.

As I turned around to avoid eye contact, he reached for me and began to roughly grope my body. In the seconds it took for the CCTV to notify security, he completely dominated me as I did everything in my attempt to scream and desperately break free. The room spun around me, a blur of neon lights and shadows, as I struggled against his unwanted advances. Seconds stretched into eternity before security burst in, but by then the damage had been done. He had taken something deeply personal from me—the feeling of safety and my belief in my own invulnerability.

That night marked a turning point. I understood that the risks of this profession went far beyond what I had imagined. The glittering world of the club, which had once seemed like a path to easy money and excitement, now revealed the depths of its dark nature. The question now was: How would I move forward from here? Could I find a way to heal, to reclaim my sense of self and safety? Or would this one moment forever define me, trapping me in a cycle of fear of men, of touch, of intimacy?

It was because of this horrific night that I sought answers, driven by a need to understand what was happening not just to me, but to the women who shared my reality. I learned trauma doesn't just live in our memories—it can lodge itself in our bodies. It was in the pages of *The Body Keeps the Score* by Dr. Bessel van der Kolk, a pioneering researcher in the field of trauma, where he shares that traumatic experiences literally reshape both body and brain, compromising sufferers' capacities for pleasure, engagement, self-control, and trust.

Suddenly, it made sense. The constant state of hypervigilance many of us found ourselves in—always on edge, always ready for potential danger—was our body's way of trying to protect us from threats we had already lived through and ones we feared were yet to come.

Chloe, the veteran dancer who had confided in me about seeing her ex-husband, began experiencing panic attacks. "It's like my body remembers things my mind wants to forget," she told me one night as we passed time sharing deep stories and truths that we both commonly hid from the world. The trauma of her abusive marriage, compounded by the nightly objectification she experienced at the club, had created a perfect storm in her nervous system that one simply couldn't out-dance.

But it wasn't just the obvious traumas that affected us. Dr. Peter Levine, another expert in the field, talks about how even seemingly minor stressors, when accumulated over time, can result in nervous system dysregulation.[1] The constant judgment of our bodies, the emotional labor of manufacturing desire and intimacy, the late nights and disrupted sleep patterns, all added up to create a toxic load that our systems struggled to process.

For many of us, the trauma we experienced at the club became intertwined with earlier life experiences, creating complex layers of wounding. I felt permanently on guard at the club, with its

---

[1] Peter A. Levine, *Waking the Tiger: Healing Trauma* (North Atlantic Books, 1997).

unpredictable clients and charged atmosphere, always on the lookout for danger, keeping my nervous system in a constant state of arousal. It was a survival mechanism I had carried with me since childhood. The club only turned the volume up, keeping my body in a perpetual state of fight-or-flight.

When trauma goes unaddressed, it doesn't simply disappear. Instead, it manifests in various ways, often when we least expect it. Some dancers, like myself, struggled with forming healthy relationships outside of work, finding it difficult to trust or to separate genuine intimacy from performance. Others developed addictive behaviors, using substances or engaging in risky activities to numb the pain or to feel a sense of control. Boundaries were a constant battle to maintain, both at work and in our personal lives. The ongoing violation of our physical and emotional space at the club bled into other areas, making it hard to assert ourselves or to recognize when our limits were being crossed.

For me, so much of my trauma healed itself through writing. Writing forced me to reconstruct memories that were fragmented, from times in which I struggled to find wholeness. The memories that emerged as I mentally sifted through my past and put pen to paper were filled with themes of dissociation. I soon realized I was trying to reconcile different parts of myself that didn't seem to naturally fit together, like pieces that belonged to different puzzles. Through writing, I eventually processed what my conscious mind at the time of those painful events couldn't fully grapple with and had silenced.

The journey of healing from trauma is not linear, and for many of us, it's ongoing. But in acknowledging the impact of our experiences, in seeking understanding and support, we are taking accountability and reclaiming our wholeness one step, or one word, at a time.

CHAPTER 8

LOST IS A LOVELY PLACE TO FIND YOURSELF

One evening, before the usual chaos swallowed the night, I found myself sitting across from Amber in the club's restaurant, sharing a quiet meal between shifts. She was a dancer who'd been there longer than anyone else. She toyed with her fork absentmindedly before finally speaking up.

"You know," she said, her eyes disconnected and distant, "I sometimes wonder who I'd be if I hadn't started dancing. Would I still be me? Or have I become someone else entirely?"

Her question struck me deeply, as, truthfully, I didn't have the answers. Even now, it remains a question I ask myself. One life decision—not just for Amber but for me—had created a trauma so deep I had unknowingly altered not just my path but also how people perceived me, and eventually, how I saw myself. There was a reason I told my friends I was bartending. I knew that people outside of the club life would not look kindly on my line of work. But were they right in their judgments? I realize my decision to become a dancer was and likely is still controversial—but it is also a piece of my story.

Amber's words still resonate deeply with me when I consider the implications and scrutiny I face as a result of my past. I contemplate all the personas I've adopted in this life, all the fake stories I've told and been told. Where does the performance end and the real me begin? And yet, this question isn't unique to dancers. A dancer in a strip club, a man in a suit in a boardroom, two people in a restaurant on a date—these are all places where identities blur and are carefully curated to fit the desires of the people sitting across from us. What made the club perhaps somewhat different, though, was that it never let up. It was a world of constant performance. And, after performing hour after hour, night after night, the lines between the real and the constructed selves began to dissolve. After a few months at the club, the act of slipping into a role, while initially a means of survival, had become second nature to me, leaving me questioning the authenticity of my interactions and even myself.

My mind drifted, as it often did, to childhood—the deep pain of my father leaving, engulfed in a vivid memory of me chasing him down the paved street I grew up on, my small legs desperate to keep up as he disappeared around a corner. That sense of rejection is a wound that has never fully healed, compounded by the loss of familiarity as we uprooted from the UK to Ireland in search of a better life and a fresh start, which had instead felt like another layer of loss. The abandonment of my father and the subsequent move taught me from a very young age that safety and a picture-perfect life were not promised like it seemed to be in the fairytales or children's books I'd read as a little girl. The comfort I'd known from an intact family and our relative stability in the

UK was stripped away from one day to the next, replaced by the harsh reality of starting over in a new country and watching my mother battle through each day, her strength a double-edged sword that both lifted and pressed down on me. It weighs on me still to this day.

Her sacrifices were a demonstration of her love, but they also underscored the void left by my father's absence, a void that no amount of resilience could completely fill. My mother's attempt at playing two roles and the emotional drinking she soothed herself with were a constant backdrop to my formative years. Her strength in the face of hardship was both inspiring and heartbreaking. The later betrayal by my new stepfather, who cheated and eventually left, only deepened my distrust of men and sense of insecurity.

My childhood was tainted by an inescapable sense of longing and alienation, masked by a family divided by unseen boundaries and disapproval. Now in Ireland, my mother met someone new: Peter. They married when I was five, soon after the birth of my brother. Peter was an Irishman with deep-rooted cultural ties, and I see my mother's marriage to him as a desperate attempt at normalcy in a world that seemed intent on rejecting her. But Peter's family, a close-knit Catholic clan wary of outsiders, struggled to accept my mother's English background and my existence as a child from a previous relationship. From the earliest days, I felt the heaviness of their disapproval. I was a reminder of a past they'd rather forget, a blemish on their immaculate family lineage.

The addition of my brothers marked a turning point: I saw the reflection of the family I could never truly be a part of and became aware of the unspoken past that separated me from my siblings. They were the embodiment of Peter's Irish legacy, carrying forward a heritage and a family pride that I could only observe from the sidelines. This awareness fed into a growing belief that I was somehow lacking, not good enough to be fully embraced for who I was. I internalized this feeling, linking it to the absence of my biological father. In my young mind, these two facts became intertwined—I wasn't enough for my father to stay, and I wasn't enough for my new family to fully accept me. This narrative took root, shaping my self-perception for years to come, until a revelatory moment at the age of twenty-nine forced me to confront the truth I had long avoided.

Peter himself was a product of his generation and upbringing, a man who wore his stoicism like a shield. Emotions were a foreign language to him, one he seemed to have no interest in learning. His approach to fatherhood was defined by strict rules and high expectations, which were passed down from his father, with little room for the softer aspects of parenting. His love, if you could call it that, was not a given but a prize to be earned through obedience and academic achievement. As a child, I found myself constantly striving for his approval, reaching for a connection that always seemed just out of grasp. I questioned what secrets lay hidden behind those iron eyes. What wounds festered beneath his stoic exterior? The weight of unasked questions and his emotional distance created a tension in our household, a barrier that I never quite learned how to breach.

As I grew older, I often found myself wondering about the forces that had shaped Peter into the man he was. Was it the weight of religious doctrine, drilled into him from an early age, that hardened him? Or perhaps the societal pressures of his time, demanding that men be unwavering providers, devoid of visible emotion or vulnerability? These questions swirled in my mind, unspoken and unanswered, adding layers of complexity to our already strained relationship. Despite the challenges, there were rare moments when I caught glimpses of something softer in Peter—a quick look of pride, a joint sing-along in the car before pulling into the drive and the momentary happiness left on the road. These moments were few and far between, but they fueled a persistent hope that somehow, someday, we might form a connection. However, as I grew older, so did the distance between us.

I made the decision to leave high school abruptly, at the age of sixteen. It was never what I might have imagined myself doing when I was younger, but it felt like my only escape from a system that seemed designed to control rather than to empower. As I walked out of that school for the last time, the world suddenly seemed vast and intimidating, full of possibilities and pitfalls in equal measure. In the years that followed, I watched as my former classmates continued their structured journey toward adulthood. Their lives seemed to follow a predetermined path—exams, university applications, and part-time jobs at local shops. But I knew I couldn't stay on that path. I needed a getaway plan and fast.

With a heart full of determination and a suitcase stuffed with dreams and ballet tights, I fled to Barcelona. Over the course of my life, dance had always been my sanctuary, the one thing I knew I could do well after years of competitive training. It was my ticket out, away from the suffocating atmosphere of home, where, after my mother's marriage with Peter fell apart, her misguided attempts at reclaiming her lost youth had entangled her with men sometimes barely older than me. It had created a twisted, uncomfortable dynamic, and so I ran, seeking solace in the unknown. As I navigated the unfamiliar Spanish streets, a worn map clutched tightly in hand, I felt my past slowly lifting off my shoulders. Here, I was unburdened by history. Nobody knew me. There were no preconceived notions about who I was or what I could become. The anonymity was liberating, exhilarating even. For the first time in my life, I felt truly free to define myself on my own terms. I had no concrete plan beyond my determination to make it as a dancer. My savings were meager, my Spanish rudimentary at best. But at eighteen, these seemed like minor obstacles.

I found myself sharing a cramped one-bedroom apartment with Isabelle, a vivacious Irish girl I'd met in Dublin who had spontaneously decided to join in on the adventure as an attempt not just to escape her environment but herself. My "bedroom" was a makeshift space in the hallway, barely accommodating a mattress, but it felt like a palace of possibility. Living with Isabelle was like watching a beautiful, haunting dance unfold in real time. Her long limbs and delicate frame moved through our tiny apartment with a grace that seemed at odds with the pain I sensed within. God, she was talented in a way that left me in awe. At night, I would sit on our ratty sofa chair, mesmerized, as she practiced in the narrow space between our kitchenette and the wall. Watching her dance was like witnessing joy and pain intertwined. She danced with a rawness that could break your heart and mend it in the same breath.

But there were darker dances too. The quiet step of her feet to the bathroom late at night. The sound of the faucet running way too long, and the way she pushed food around on her plate at dinner, barely touching it. I wanted to say something. Anything. But the words always stuck in my throat. What right did I have? We were just two girls playing at being grown-ups in a foreign city. Who was I to point out the cracks in her carefully choreographed performance when I was barely holding my own life together? I wondered if my silence made me just as much a prisoner as her demons did her. So, we both kept up the act.

Laughter bounced off the thin walls as we navigated this new life as two girls against the world, making up our own rules as we went along in this sun-soaked city by the sea.

Our days were filled with the rigorous demands of dance training, the grueling routines, and hours spent in the studio were both physically and mentally exhausting. The evening, however, was a place of discovery—fumbling through recipes in our tiny kitchen, which became the stage for our cooking experiments, often laughing at our disasters and reveling in the small victories of adulthood as we bonded over burned paella and soggy tortillas. Money was scarce, but happiness was abundant. We would sit on the balcony, icing our aching and bruised bodies before swapping our pointe shoes for knee-high combat boots, ready to step into the night like we owned it.

The city's magic truly came alive in the arms of our Spanish lovers. They swept into our lives like characters from romance films, with their passionate demeanor and adventurous gestures. Izzy's fiery boyfriend, Marco, was a whirlwind of intensity, and their relationship was a storm of heated arguments, sex, and passionate reconciliation. Meanwhile, my own temporary lover, Danny, the barista from the café across the way from our apartment, was far softer. Every morning, I would sit on my balcony, coffee in hand, as we flirted from a distance, our eyes meeting across the narrow street. His smile was a promise of the night to come, a secret shared just between us.

Impromptu Vespa rides through winding streets filled me with a sense of freedom, the wind in my hair and my arms wrapped tightly around his toned waist. Nights stretched into dawn as we watched the sun rise over the Mediterranean Sea, sand between our toes and the taste of cheap alcohol on our lips. Those moments felt eternal, like a dream that I never wanted to wake up from, now memories that barely feel real. Our time together was a young love story—never destined to go anywhere but rich with heady infatuation as we experienced life fully present in every moment. We'd spend hours wrapped up in each other, high on love and weed as we forgot the world outside, sharing deep conversations that would last hours and hours. It was as though we both knew it wouldn't last forever, so we cherished every fleeting second.

Izzy and I would lose ourselves for hours among the crowds as Las Ramblas, a pedestrian thoroughfare lined with trees, shops, and restaurants, became our playground. We were captivated by street performers and seduced by the aromas wafting in the warm air from tiny tapas bars. Every corner held the promise of a new experience, a new friend, or a new piece of ourselves waiting to be found. We danced with strangers in bars, sang with buskers in lanes, and let the vibrant chaos of the city fill us with every sense of the meaning of life. The sounds, smells, and sights of Barcelona became a part of me, embedding themselves in my memory forever.

But as our dance program neared its end, reality began to creep in, and the looming question of "What next?" hung over us both, revealing the fragility of the life we'd created. Faced with this crossroads, I did what any aspiring dancer with stars in her eyes and fire in her soul would do—I set my sights on the stage. Izzy made her way to the infamous stage of the Moulin Rouge in Paris. As for me, I heard the West End call my name. Its bright lights and legendary musical theatre productions promised the fulfillment of my deepest dreams. With a mix of apprehension and excitement within me, I bid farewell to the beginning of adulthood in Barcelona and the carefree girl I'd been there. I stepped onto my next path, knowing that the pursuit of dreams often requires leaving a piece of yourself behind.

The decision to move to London was both impulsive and inevitable, as if it had been written in my heart long before I arrived. I came with little more than a small suitcase full of black leotards and a relentless hunger to make it. The city was everything I'd imagined and more—a pulsing, spirited entity that made anything feel possible. The towering skyscrapers and bustling streets teeming with life and luxury felt both inspiring and defeating all at once.

But London, I quickly learned, was not a fairy godmother waiting to grant wishes. It was a city of grit, demanding everything I had and then asking for more. The cost of living was staggering, and I found myself wedged in a tiny room in a shared house of foreign students, all of us chasing our own versions of success. The city never slept and neither did my worries. I had landed in a place where my dreams and desires quickly collided with the stark reality of survival and struggle.

I threw myself into the hustle, working two, sometimes three jobs just to keep my head above water, all while auditioning for shows and taking dance classes in any spare time that I had. During the day, I'd serve coffee to harried office workers in Covent Garden or fold clothes and contemplate life in the stockroom of a high-class store. At night, I'd manage the guest list for one of the most sought-after clubs in Chelsea, watching as people with more money than I'd ever seen spent it freely on overpriced bottles and tables. Night after night, I stood in the front line of the vetting process, my fingers numb with cold yet never breaking the act that I was someone of importance.

There were moments when I felt truly alive, caught up in the energy and potential of London. The bright lights, the constant motion, the sense that anything could happen—it was intoxicating and enough to keep the dream alive. But there were also dark nights when the reality of my decisions and the unrelenting struggle threatened to crush me after another rejection from an audition.

It was during one of these low points that I stumbled into the underground rave scene. A coworker invited me along as an escape from the daily grind. The first time I stepped into one of these hidden events was like entering another world. The music, the press of bodies, the mesmerizing lights—it all combined to create a sensory overload that drowned out the constant chatter of my doubts and fears. And then there were the drugs. The high became an escape, the dance floor a place where I could lose myself and forget my troubles. For those few euphoric hours, lost in the crowd and the beat, I could forget about the girl who dropped out of school, who didn't fit in, who was alone in the world, who was barely scraping by. I could be anyone, or no one at all. It was addictive, this feeling of release, and I found myself seeking it out more and more often. Each rave was a temporary escape, a chance to reclaim a part of myself that felt lost in the everyday grind of survival.

But as the sun rose and the music faded, reality always came crashing back. I'd sit slumped on the morning tube, ears ringing and mind buzzing with the remnants of a high that never lasted long enough. I'd snatch a few hours of sleep before dragging myself out of bed to start the cycle all over again. In those quiet moments, as the city slowly awoke outside my window, I'd often find myself wondering: Was this the life I'd imagined when I left school? Was I moving forward, or just running in place? The contrast between the night's freedom and the day's constraints left me questioning my path—if I was even on a path at all.

The girl who had left her small Irish town with big dreams felt lost in the vastness of London and life. Yet, even in my darkest moments, a stubborn spark of hope refused to be extinguished. Somewhere in this city, I believed, was the key to unlocking my potential, to proving everyone who had doubted me—including myself—wrong. I just had to find it, no matter the cost.

Sitting with Amber that night, I thought of the girl who had so bravely moved to London, I felt the same pride as I did back then. I'd come to a city alone, with no money and no friends. And here I was, financially stable. Taking care of myself. Amber had said, "I sometimes wonder who I'd be if I hadn't started dancing." But for now, I wasn't looking back and wondering, but looking forward, waiting for my story to unfold as I sat in my lingerie and heels, ready to step onto the floor and let the story continue.

CHAPTER 9

CAN YOU OUT-HUSTLE A HUSTLER?

The transformation of my worldview stretched far beyond my work as my life took on an almost surreal quality. The financial struggles and scarcity I faced when I first moved to London had faded, replaced by a new way of living and sense of control. My social life evaporated, consumed by the nocturnal world I now belonged to in the club, while my interest in men outside the professional realm withered—a casualty of what I had come to witness night after night.

My views on men didn't shift suddenly, but in a gradual erosion, shaped by what I saw and felt. Every eager face, every wedding ring that seemed to lose its significance in the dark of the night, contributed to my rising walls of distrust. The absurd amounts of cash I would be offered in exchange for a night's company became a grim testament to the fragility of human fidelity. I saw how what once might have been dismissed as isolated incidents began to form a recurring pattern in many men, a story of broken promises and shattered vows. Each transaction, each whispered confession, illuminated vulnerabilities and weaknesses—the relentless pursuit of fleeting satisfaction that colors the human condition. It was a depressing reality.

In the darkness of the night, I witnessed the polarity between outward appearances and inner chaos. By day, these men held power and poise; by night, they would strip away their facades in these intimate settings. The same men who commanded boardrooms and courtrooms would reveal their deepest insecurities, unmet needs, and wildest fantasies, too raw to name, which still unsettles me today. The backroom became a confession box, a place where the protective layer of strength was peeled back to expose the raw, unfiltered human experience. Here, the cultural narratives about masculinity and success could lead individuals to seek validation in the most transient and superficial of ways.

The club wasn't about mere physical attraction; it was about the promise of escape, of being seen and heard in ways that everyday life often denied. For many of these men, the club offered a temporary reprieve from the pressures of conformity, a space where they could express parts of themselves that were otherwise suppressed. Nightly, I found myself grappling with a mix of empathy and cynicism. I could see the pain behind the charm, the loneliness masked as confidence, and who was I to judge? It was easy to label these men as unfaithful or weak, but the truth was far more complex. Just like me, they were victims of their choices and circumstances, caught in a web of societal pressure and personal insecurities, where we would betray our deepest values in the pursuit of momentary gratification. Beneath it all, we were all searching for something—validation, love, a sense of belonging.

Self-reflection led me to consider that communication could pave the way for deeper, more meaningful connections. Many of these men sought refuge in the club because they felt misunderstood or unappreciated at home. Yet, perhaps if they had chosen to communicate openly with their spouses rather than seeking superficial validation from strangers, they might have discovered paths to genuine intimacy. Of course, this was easier said than done. Addressing the root causes of their behavior would require them to confront the societal constructs that dictate masculinity and success. Often, these men were trapped in roles demanding constant strength and stoicism, leaving little room for emotional expression. Not everyone was ready to do that work. But if they could find the courage to challenge those norms, they could foster a more balanced approach to their identities, one that embraces emotional intelligence and vulnerability as strengths rather than weaknesses.

This change could help break the cycles of disconnection and infidelity that plague so many relationships. Vulnerable, open-hearted conversations with their partners could set a precedent for their children and communities, promoting honesty and emotional health. When both partners feel valued and heard, we build a society that prioritizes genuine connection over superficial appearances. This creates the foundation for more resilient, fulfilling relationships.

Though these ideas were taking on a clear shape in my head at the time, I never spoke of it to my customers. I felt that I could see a better path forward for them, but advising them to be more honest with their spouses or encouraging them to redefine their masculinity were not what they were at the club to get from me. So I kept my observations to myself.

One particular client, Simon, always left a lasting impression on me. A high-powered lawyer from Denmark, he had piercing blue eyes that seemed to see straight through me and meticulously combed back hair that spoke of his perfectionism. Every month, like clockwork, Simon would appear, slipping into his usual seat as if he were seeking refuge. On one occasion, as he settled into the plush chair across from me, Simon exhaled deeply, as if the weight of his own world had just landed on his shoulders.

"You know, Heather," he began, his voice tinged with frustration, "my wife just doesn't get me. She's always so wrapped up in her own world."

He leaned in slightly, his hand brushing mine with a slow touch that felt more intimate than intended. "She's not the person I thought she'd be," he continued, his eyes searching mine for a flicker of understanding.

I nodded, my gaze shifting to his hand still lingering on my arm. I couldn't help but wonder about the woman waiting at home, oblivious to the secrets he carried and the money he spent on these escapades. Her image materialized in my mind—a woman of patience, of quiet devotion, someone who had likely once believed the promises he had made her.

As Simon spoke, I saw the duality of his character—his desperate need for approval, and the way his tales of marital discord played out as if scripted for an audience that included me. I was drawn to him, despite knowing the pain it would bring. His disloyalty, his stories, became a twisted form of validation, a reflection of my own unresolved wounds. I believe now that he mirrored my father's perpetual unavailability. The familiarity of his approval, however flawed, was both a painful reminder and an allure I couldn't easily escape.

As my time at the club progressed, the romantic ideals I once cherished—visions of finding a perfect partner or experiencing a fairytale love—no longer held any appeal. In the world of the club, where every interaction was negotiated, these notions I had once held so dear seemed naive and out of place. The dreams of a loving relationship had been replaced by the reality of transactional affection. The more I immersed myself in this world, the more distant those ideals seemed, as if they had belonged to someone else entirely. Each night, I perfected the art of detachment, my heart becoming as guarded as the VIP rooms we danced in. Somewhere along the way, I stopped believing in the kind of love I had once longed for.

Each night, I danced a complex routine with clients, a dance of seduction and illusion. We moved to the rhythm set by unspoken rules and expectations, our steps a delicate balance of intimacy and distance. This nightly performance crept into my perception of all relationships, making it difficult for me to remember how to relate to people outside this scripted environment. I began to see every interaction through the lens of the club, questioning the sincerity of smiles and the authenticity of compliments. The real world started to feel like an extension of my nightly performances, a place where masks were worn, and true intentions were hidden beneath layers of practiced charisma.

But the cherished visions of romantic love weren't the only ideals of mine that deteriorated over time. Stepping into the club felt like stepping outside the usual social script, and with that came a growing awareness. I began to critically examine the pursuit of wealth and status, wondering if these commonly accepted goals truly led to fulfillment or simply masked a deeper emptiness. The concept of social comparison became particularly relevant, as I observed how individuals constantly measured themselves against others, often to their own detriment, just like dancers did each night between one another. I saw the same patterns of insecurity and competition in the polished, high-powered clients as I did in the brightly lit dressing rooms where dancers sized each other up, calculating who was making the most money, who was getting the most attention, and who had secured the most lucrative regular. Meanwhile, in boardrooms, powerful men played the same game by competing in a silent battle of status, flashing their Rolexes, buying the most expensive cars, seeking validation in the approval of those around them. The only real difference between the two worlds was the setting. This relentless comparison created a culture of dissatisfaction and envy, where true contentment was always just out of reach, overshadowed by someone else's perceived success.

Paradoxically, the world I had crafted for myself in the club felt both secure and liberating.

Yes, it had changed me, and perhaps even harmed some parts of me, giving me a guarded view of relationships and instilling new fears in me. But it was also a stage of my own design, where I controlled the music and the steps. Here, I shielded myself from the harsh truths about love and human nature, dancing to my own tune in a performance that never truly ended. I was the director, the star, and the audience, all at once. The vulnerability of opening to real emotions was replaced by the comfort of predictable roles and outcomes. My life had become a series of well-rehearsed acts, where the boundaries were clear and the risks were minimized. And while this world offered something that resembled control, it also kept me from the raw, unfiltered experiences that lay beyond the stage, perpetuating a cycle of isolation and superficiality.

Days melted into one another as I explored the streets of London, a solitary figure drifting in and out of high-end shops and dining at the finest establishments. The ability to enter luxury stores without financial concerns added another layer to my unusual life experiences. It was a journey of extremes. I'd sit for hours in hidden cafés, observing the ebb and flow of city life, feeling both apart from and a part of the bustling world around me. I found a peculiar comfort in my anonymity among the crowds, each street and alleyway holding its own secrets, and I reveled in the freedom to explore them without restraint. The contrast between my solitary wandering and the city's relentless pace heightened my awareness of the many lives intersecting with mine, even if only for fleeting moments.

The psychological impact of my experiences began to manifest in unexpected ways. I found myself increasingly drawn to observing and analyzing human behavior, not just in the club but in everyday interactions. This heightened awareness led me to question the underlying motivations driving people's actions and decisions. Each interaction became a mystery to unravel; I scraped at the hidden layers of emotion and tried to perceive people's true intentions beneath the surface. The more nights I worked, the more I realized how much people struggled to reconcile their desires with their realities, a struggle I knew all too well. My fascination with human behavior grew, becoming an unspoken study that occupied my thoughts and colored my perceptions of the world around me.

I noticed how people, myself included, often lived with contradictions—holding beliefs in one moment, then acting in ways that clashed with them. It was a silent struggle inside, a tension between who we wanted to be and the realities we faced. This cognitive dissonance seemed especially prevalent in the corporate world, where professionals frequently compromised their personal ethics in pursuit of career advancement or financial gain. I watched as suited professionals hurried between gleaming skyscrapers, their faces a mix of determination and barely concealed stress. These individuals, I realized, were often trapped in a cycle of ambition and expectation. Their pursuit of success, while admirable, seemed to come at the cost of personal fulfillment and genuine human connection.

Contrasting this corporate frenzy, I found solace in Kensington Gardens. Here, amid the tranquil ponds and ancient trees, I observed a different rhythm of life. Families picnicked on weekends, artists sketched quietly by themselves, and elderly couples strolled hand in hand. These scenes of simple joy and connection soothed my soul after the chaotic energy of the financial district, highlighting the diverse ways people try to find meaning in their lives. The park became a sanctuary for me, a place where time seemed to slow down, and the pressures of the outside world faded into the background. Here, I wasn't Heather or Jade. I could breathe freely, allowing myself to be present in the moment and appreciate the beauty of life's simpler pleasures. The disparity between the park's serenity, the corporate world's relentless drive, and the chaos of the club underscored the duality of existence, reminding me that balance was essential for true fulfillment. And yet, as much as I treasured these moments of stillness, they also deepened the divide within me. If this was peace, why did it seem perpetually out of reach?

Despite the turmoil, I started to witness the growth within me. In the high-stakes environment of the club, I had honed my ability to read and respond to others' emotions. However, I began to recognize the importance of applying these skills in all areas of life, not just in professional settings. This led me to explore ways of developing greater empathy and improving my interpersonal relationships later in life. Emotional intelligence became a cornerstone of my personal growth, allowing me to navigate complex social dynamics with greater ease and understanding. The ability to connect with others on a deeper level not only enhanced my relationships but also provided a sense of fulfillment that had been lacking in my life. It was a revelation that the same skills I used to thrive in the club could also help me build more meaningful connections outside of it.

As I continue my spiritual journey and my understanding of human behavior expands, I find myself grappling with deeper existential questions. What truly gives life meaning? Is happiness a realistic goal, or should we strive for something else, like contentment or purpose? These questions have led me to explore various philosophical frameworks, psychological theories, and ancient spiritual traditions about the nature of human existence. The search for answers became a personal quest, guiding me through different mystery schools of thought and practices. I have immersed myself in the works and practices of indigenous shamans, esoteric teaching, and Jungian psychology, seeking wisdom in their words and lineage. From the shaman's connection to the unseen to the psychologist's analysis of the subconscious, I have found pieces of truth that resonate among different traditions. Each new theory or ancient ritual has added another layer to my understanding, helping me piece together a more cohesive picture of what it meant to live a meaningful life and find peace with those bigger life questions.

The question of identity has also become a central theme in my reflections. In a world where we often define ourselves by our professions, relationships, or social roles, what constitutes our true self? Ever since those days at the club, I have pondered the concept of self-actualization and the challenges of achieving authenticity in a society that often rewards conformity and performance. One thing is sure: It is not for the faint of heart. It requires a relentless commitment to peeling back illusions and confronting uncomfortable truths.

The more I explore these psychological and existential questions, the more I realize how much remains a mystery about the human mind and experience. This recognition of the vastness of human complexity and the limitations of our current understanding has given me a permanent sense of humility and curiosity. It reinforces the idea that the journey of self-discovery and psychological exploration is always ongoing, with each answer uncovering new questions to be explored.

Between sleep and work, in quiet moments alone, I was unwittingly building a stronger, more resilient version of myself. From juggling low-wage jobs to newfound independence, my perspective on what mattered was shifting. Amid the bustling chaos of London, where anonymity reigned, I discovered a surprising solace. The deviation from my past of juggling multiple minimum wage jobs heightened the surreal nature of my new reality. This contrast between a life of luxury and my origins has granted me a distinct perspective on what truly matters in life.

London's frenetic energy, with its relentlessness and unspoken disconnection, mirrored the internal tumult I felt. Watching people battle their way onto the underground, with their culture of constant, spiritually bankrupting hustling, and how they single-mindedly chased power, success, and external validation that can only be found within, made a huge impression on me. Observing all that energy that people frantically poured into things that could not ultimately satisfy prompted me to reassess my values and priorities. I questioned everything I had once believed.

If wealth and power were the ultimate goals, why did so many people who possessed them seem just as lost as those without? The daily grind, while impressive in its intensity, seemed hollow and devoid of genuine fulfillment.

We live in a world where slowing down feels almost impossible.

The pervasive "hustle culture" that dominates modern society is deeply rooted in our evolutionary past and societal structures. Our ancestors' survival depended on constant vigilance and hard work, a trait that has been reinforced by capitalist ideologies promising success through relentless effort. While this mindset fosters innovation and progress, it frequently comes at the expense of our mental and spiritual well-being. The ceaseless push for productivity and achievement creates an atmosphere where rest is seen as weakness and self-worth is tied to output.

Psychologically, hustle culture preys on our inherent need for validation and belonging. It taps into the deep-seated fear of not being good enough unless we are constantly achieving and improving. This relentless culture of constant comparison—where success is measured by titles, salaries, and online presence—feeds an insatiable hunger for approval and recognition. It generates a psychological environment where self-worth is linked to external accomplishments, leading to a cycle of achievement addiction. We find ourselves on a hedonic treadmill, forever chasing the next goal without ever feeling truly satisfied.

Think of how we often pursue the next promotion, the next purchase, or the next big life milestone, believing it will finally make us happy. The transient nature of these rewards means that true contentment remains elusive. Each new milestone reached quickly loses its significance, overshadowed by the next goal on the horizon. The more we chase these external markers of success, the more we risk losing touch with our inner values and desires, leading to a profound sense of emptiness and a crisis of identity.

This unrelenting pursuit also creates a disconnect between our actions and our core values. Individuation is the process of becoming one's true self, which stands in direct opposition to the conformity often demanded by hustle culture. When we constantly focus on external success, we risk alienation, a sense of estrangement from our own life and work. This alienation can manifest as a hollow feeling, where even our greatest accomplishments feel empty because they are not aligned with our true desires and values. Because, at its core, hustle culture is not just about working harder; it's about shaping ourselves to fit expectations that may not even be our own. The more we conform, the harder it becomes to remember who we truly are.

The concept of soul alignment—finding one's true path— draws from various philosophical and psychological traditions. In simple terms, it's about living in a way that feels right not just in your head, but in your heart and spirit. It's similar to Abraham Maslow's idea of self-actualization, or reaching one's full potential, and the Buddhist concept of "right livelihood," where work is in harmony with ethical principles and personal values. Achieving this level of alignment means slowing down enough to reflect on who you really are, what truly matters to you, and having the courage to diverge from societal expectations. It's not just about asking what we want to achieve, but why we want to achieve it— and whether those ambitions genuinely feed our deeper needs and desires.

Reframing our approach to life and success necessitates a paradigm shift—a fundamental change in the way we see and respond to the world around us and within us. Rather than viewing challenges as obstacles to be overcome through sheer force of will, we can see them as opportunities for growth and self-discovery. This perspective aligns with post-traumatic growth theory, which, at its core, is the idea that difficult or painful experiences can sometimes lead to deeper personal strength, new outlooks, and a greater appreciation for life. The practice of setting boundaries and saying no to things that don't align with our values is crucial in this process. By honoring our own needs and limits, we create space for more meaningful pursuits and relationships. This shift moves us from a mindset of scarcity—where we feel we must do everything to succeed—to one of abundance, where we focus on what truly matters.

Rejecting hustle culture doesn't mean giving up on ambition or abandoning the drive to work hard. Rather, it involves redefining success on our own terms. This shift requires developing a strong sense of self-worth that isn't dependent on external achievements. I remember a time during my early years in London when the relentless pursuit of success had me on edge. I was constantly working, striving to prove myself, and yet, I felt an emptiness persist within me.

Learning to live life with more self-compassion showed me that treating myself with kindness, rather than harsh self-criticism, leads to greater motivation and resilience. I began to prioritize activities that nourished my soul—moments of quiet reflection, simple joys like a walk through a park, and connections with friends who reminded me of my worth beyond achievements. By nurturing myself, I built a foundation of inner strength that allowed me to pursue my goals with a sense of joy and fulfillment, rather than out of fear or obligation.

This approach to life—prioritizing internal alignment over external hustle—became the key to unlocking a new way of living. For so long, I had operated in a constant state of fight-or-flight, my nervous system wired for survival, conditioned to stay alert at all times. The years I spent at the club had reinforced this hypervigilance, making it difficult to ever fully relax, to trust that I was safe. Unlearning that took time.

The turning point for me took place during a retreat I attended in Bali, where I was introduced to mindfulness and self-compassion. It was there that I truly felt, for the first time, the difference between the frantic energy of hustle and the calm of being connected with my true self. The effects of that moment were far-reaching, but one of them was that I started to view work as less of a chore and more of a natural expression of my talents and passions.

I noticed that when I started making choices that felt true to me, even the smallest ones—a conversation spoken honestly, a decision guided by my values—they had effects that reached beyond just my own life. This shift in perspective influenced more than my inner world. As I began valuing authentic living over blind ambition, I saw a broader impact on my relationships, career choices, and overall sense of purpose. Turning my focus inward and paying attention to my growth as a woman, I started advocating for sustainable practices at work and sought roles that aligned with my values rather than just monetary success. I've done a lot of work on myself, but I'm dreaming bigger, imagining a society where well-being is valued as much as wealth, and where people are encouraged to follow paths that truly reflect who they are, not just what they're told to pursue.

Moving away from hustle culture toward a more aligned way of living isn't just about personal well-being—it's about reimagining how we as a society approach work, success, and the very meaning of a life well-lived. It's a journey of reclaiming our time, energy, and ultimately, our humanity in an increasingly demanding world. This transformation begins with individual choices but has the potential to reshape our communities and our world, creating a more compassionate and fulfilling way of life for everyone.

Had I known during my time at the club what I know now, after years of self-discovery and growth, I often wonder how different my path might have been. Would I have made the same choices, ended up where I am today? Or did I need to lose myself in order to truly find my way? Was every twist and turn, every heartbreak and triumph, an essential part of the journey that led me here, or could I have arrived with fewer wounds, fewer regrets?

I hold a deep compassion for my younger self—the girl who stepped into the unknown with naive courage, mistaking survival for freedom. She embraced each experience as it came, wide-eyed and reckless, believing she had control over a world that was, in reality, shaping her more than she ever shaped it. Was she the one hustling the world, or was the world hustling her? The lines blur in hindsight, but what I do know is this: Those early days were only the beginning. The real challenges—the ones that would force me to confront every illusion I had built about myself— were yet to unfold. Life would push me to my limits and beyond, testing not just my resilience but my willingness to let go of who I thought I had to be in order to become who I was meant to be.

CHAPTER 10

NO RISK, NO LOVE

Life is full of moments we rarely notice until they're gone. We never know when it's going to be the last time we see someone, the last time we hear their voice, or the last time their presence lingers in a room we once shared. Lucky streaks can end without warning, and even places that feel permanent can vanish from our lives. The finite nature of these once-in-a-lifetime moments has taught me to deeply appreciate every encounter for what it is: brief, fleeting, and unrepeatable. The club had a way of making that lesson painfully clear. In a place where everything felt transient, where faces blurred into each other and time passed in neon-lit fragments, I learned nothing is ever guaranteed, but anything was possible. One night could rewrite your story. One conversation, one glance across a dimly lit room, one seemingly insignificant decision, could alter the course of your life.

But what I've come to realize is that our power—our sense of who we are—can't be given away, can't be left in the hands of another person. We can't rely on someone else to save us from our own lives or our own decisions or to take responsibility for our life choices. It's up to us to figure out what we're working toward, who we're becoming, and take empowered steps toward that future. The people we meet along the way, the encounters and conversations—they're like fate's nudges, pushing us closer to that version of ourselves we're meant to be as we evolve. Sometimes, those nudges come from the most unexpected places.

One night at the club, I was standing at the bar between dances, wiping the sweat off the back of my neck. My feet were sore, but the night wasn't over yet. A client requested a private dance, and I slipped back into the mode, that carefully constructed mask I wore when I needed to be seductive and mysterious. As I stepped into the booth, I felt a strange sense of familiarity. Then I saw him—James. He sat there, waiting for me, his suit as sharp as I remembered, but this time there was something different. His eyes locked onto mine as I stepped closer, and for a heartbeat, the world outside the booth didn't exist.

"Did you miss me?" I asked, trying to lighten the mood with a flirty grin. I couldn't quite tell what kind of tension was hanging in the air—whether it was sexual or something else. The silence between us felt heavier than it should have. James didn't say anything right away. Instead, he took off his coat and draped it across the chair beside him. He looked at me with an intensity that made me feel exposed in a way that had nothing to do with what I was wearing. The club had a strict no-touching rule, but I was still in my emerald-green gown, and when he reached out to gently stroke my leg, I let him. The sensation of his fingers grazing my skin was almost comforting, and I wasn't sure why. Maybe it was the way he looked at me, like he saw someone beyond Heather.

James worked in the city in tech and, as far as I could tell, was quite successful. He exuded a level of confidence that came with knowing his way around power and money, the kind of man who had spent years mastering the art of control. His presence reminded me how attraction is not always logical—sometimes it's an energy. There was this quiet arrogance in the way he carried himself, a certainty that the world would bend to his will. And yet, despite all that success, there was something that drew him back to me. Maybe it was the allure of the club, or maybe it was something deeper—something even he couldn't fully understand. I wondered why, after all this time, he would return to see me. He could have had anyone. His wealth and position opened doors that were locked for most people, doors to women far more glamorous and far less complicated than I was. But here he was, sitting across from me, breaking the rules we both knew existed. It made me question what he was really after, whether this was about me at all or just another challenge for him to conquer.

"So, why don't you tell me why you're really here?" I leaned in close to him, my lips brushing his ear, letting my hand glide "accidentally" across his crotch. It was one of the countless tricks I had picked up over my shifts—teasing just enough to keep them hooked, without crossing the line.

James chuckled softly. "Truth is a dangerous game, Heather. Are you sure you're ready to play?"

There was something in his tone, something that made it clear this wasn't just another impulsive invitation. He stood up suddenly, his movements deliberate, like he'd just settled something within himself. "Meet me at the Portland restaurant in Marylebone at 2 p.m. tomorrow. No strings, no expectations. Just the truth."

I stared at him, my mind racing as I tried to come up with a witty reply. Meeting a client outside the club was against every rule I'd set for myself when I started dancing. No personal contact.

No real names. No connections. But something about this invitation felt different, and as he walked out of the booth, I couldn't find the words to reply or resist the sense that this was a moment to test the boundaries of trust and curiosity within myself.

The hours until 2 p.m. the following day stretched endlessly. I tried to sleep but found myself tossing and turning, replaying moments from the night before in my mind. I kept questioning whether I was making a mistake by agreeing to meet James outside of the club, breaking one of the few rules I had sworn to follow. By the time I finally dragged myself out of bed, my nerves were wound so tight I could feel my heart pounding in my chest. I had to keep reminding myself to breathe, to stay calm, to approach this like I would any other interaction with a client. But that was the thing—James didn't feel like a client anymore. And that terrified me.

The newly opened Michelin-starred restaurant was just a short walk from my flat, near Warren Street and the club. During the day, it felt as though the night didn't exist—sunshine on my face, a sense of freedom, and a feeling of being, well, me. As I approached the restaurant, I spotted James waiting by the door, looking as relaxed and self-assured as ever. The sight of him stirred something in me—excitement, anxiety, maybe both. He smiled when he saw me, his expression easy and warm, like we were old friends meeting for lunch instead of two strangers playing a dangerous game of truth and deceit.

Without hesitation, he wrapped his arm around my waist, a gesture that felt both intimate and possessive. I tensed, then allowed myself to relax as we walked inside together. The restaurant was elegant and understated, with white tablecloths and soft lighting that seemed a world away from the smoky haze of the club.

We were seated quickly, and I slipped into the chair across from James, suddenly hyperaware of how different this felt from the encounters we'd had before. Here, there were no roles to play, no dim lights or pounding music to distract from the rawness of the situation. I couldn't hide behind the persona I used at the club. It was just me, whoever that even was, sitting across from this man who seemed to see through all the layers I had carefully built around myself.

The first question out of his mouth was the one I had been dreading. "So, what's your real name?"

Of course he would ask that. Every man did, sooner or later. Most of the time, it was just a power play—a way for them to feel like they were special, like they had broken through some barrier I'd put up. But with James, it felt different. I wasn't sure what he was after. Was it control? Curiosity? Or something else entirely?

I hesitated for a moment before responding, my voice steady but distant. "It's Heather. I already told you."

His lips smirked softly, his eyes narrowing as if he didn't believe me. "Fine, we'll play that game." His tone was light, but his words were authoritative. He leaned in slightly, resting his elbows on the table. "So, Heather, tell me about the real you."

I could feel the pressure of his gaze, the way he was trying to peel back the layers, to get to something beneath. But what was the real me? Was it the girl who grew up in a small town, dreaming of something more than the mundane life laid out before her, dreaming of stability and belonging and acceptance? Or was it the woman who danced under neon lights, twisting her body into seductive shapes for men who never bothered to ask her more than her name?

I didn't answer right away, and James seemed content to let the silence stretch between us. He ordered for both of us.

The conversation stayed surface-level for a while—work, life in the city, little jokes about the absurdity of modern living. But beneath the lighthearted words, an undercurrent of something deeper, something unsaid, lingered between us.

As we finished our meal, I felt a shift in his energy, a hesitation that hadn't been there before. He seemed softer, less composed. He cleared his throat, his voice quieter now, as if he was weighing each word before releasing it.

"Last night," he began, his gaze steady but unreadable, "it wasn't just a transaction for me. I felt a connection when we first met, and I wanted to explore it further—if you're willing."

I hadn't expected that. I had been so prepared for this to be just another game, another power dynamic from which I would walk away unscathed, but this felt…different. The way he looked at me and the sincerity in his voice caught me off guard. And for a moment, I wasn't sure how to respond.

My mind raced with conflicting thoughts, each one pulling me in a different direction. I recognized a rare vulnerability—demonstrating how trust and openness reveal hidden dimensions. A part of me wanted to shut him down, to keep the walls high and impenetrable, to stay in control of the situation before it slipped into something unpredictable. But another part of me, the part that had been starved for something real, a deep connection beyond the surface, ached to take the risk, to see where this could lead, even if it meant letting my guard down. But I couldn't forget the reality of my life. The club, the rules I had set for myself, the boundaries I needed to keep in place. I swallowed the emotional tightening in my throat, meeting his gaze with a neutral expression.

"I need to get ready for work," I said, standing up and smoothing down my skirt, slipping back into the role I knew best. I hesitated just long enough for him to wonder before offering a small, knowing smile. "But you know where to find me."

James nodded, his eyes never leaving mine, following me as I walked away from the table and out the door. As I walked to work, my thoughts were a frenzy of uncertainty. I couldn't help but wonder if the connection I'd felt with James was real or just another performance on both our parts. But the laughter we'd shared over pretentious coffee orders, the way his eyes had softened when I spoke about my dreams of becoming a writer, and the gentle touch of his hand on my waist, all felt so tangible, so genuine.

In the uncertain dance of shadows and whispers that James and I had engaged in, I found myself pondering the paradox of intimacy and anonymity in modern connections. Each encounter seemed to hold a mirror to my soul, reflecting fragments of truth obscured by layers of perception and projection. Behind every touch, every shared glance, lay a story untold, and the truth. Was this fleeting moment a glimpse into a hidden realm where truths are laid bare, or merely another chapter in the complex narrative we weave to navigate the intricacies of desire and human connection? How could I tell one from another?

The restaurant, the meeting, the laughter shared—they all felt like pieces of a puzzle in the game of life. Each glance, each word, each touch was imbued with the promise of something more yet was laced with the quiet fear of what "more" might demand. Could this be the start of something real, a brief escape from the life I had meticulously protected? Or was it simply another illusion, a fleeting connection that would dissolve as quickly as it had appeared?

As I stepped into the familiar surroundings of the club, the clamor of music and choreographed chaos were both comforting and isolating. Here, I knew the script, knew exactly how to move, and how to perform on stage with a carefully constructed identity. But out there, with James, I was left to grapple with the rawness of my own emotions, the fragile space between longing and fear, between wanting more and knowing the cost. Growth often happens in these uncomfortable spaces.

But with no risk in life, I thought, there is no love. Had I made a mistake, walking away? Or avoided a serious pitfall?

The night unfolded with its usual rhythm as I moved through my routine. In the quiet moments between sets, I contemplated the nature of human connection. What does it mean to truly connect with another person? Is it built on shared experiences, on mutual understanding, or is it something less tangible, something that defies logic and reason? Is it an energy, a pull, an unspoken language that only certain souls recognize in each other?

As I pondered these questions, I realized that the essence of connection often lies in our willingness to expose our vulnerabilities and embrace the unknown. Hadn't I felt it here, in the club of all places? Nights when an unexpected conversation turned into something more meaningful, moments when a stranger's words revealed a depth I never anticipated. Yes, it was uncomfortable to take that first step, but so many times, the payoff had been beautiful. Genuine connection demands that we venture beyond our comfort zones, risking rejection and heartache for the possibility of profound intimacy. It is in these moments of courage and openness that we truly come alive, discovering depths of understanding and empathy that enhance our lives. Still, I wondered about James. If I should have leaped at a connection in the outside world—or if I'd been wise to retreat from something that might have never been real to begin with.

In the end, the true test may not be in finding the right answers but in daring to ask the difficult questions, to face the uncertainty with an open heart and an unguarded spirit. Life's mysteries are not meant to be solved but experienced, and it is through our willingness to explore these uncertainties that we find our greatest truths when we follow the whispers of our soul. It is a call to embrace the journey with all its twists and turns, to seek meaning not in the destination but in the process of searching itself. In this pursuit, we discover not just who we are but who we might become. To live fully is to engage with life's uncertainties, to risk, to love, and to continuously seek deeper connections. It is through this engagement that we uncover the richness of our existence and the profound beauty of the human experience.

As I finished my shift and the lights of the club began to fade into the early morning, my thoughts lingered on James. The brief encounter had left me with a profound sense of anticipation and uncertainty. The questions he had raised, the truths he hinted at, had stirred a curiosity within me. I found myself contemplating what it would mean to open to him—and if I would even see him again. His challenge had made me question not just the nature of our connection but my willingness to embrace the unknown, to take risks and pursue the deeper truths that life might hold.

CHAPTER 11

DANCING IN THE DARK

"Remember, honey," Nikki, the house mum who had taken a strange liking to me had said in a tone that demanded both trust and attention. "They're not just paying for the show. They're paying for the fantasy. Give them a taste of what they think they want, but always keep a part of yourself hidden."

I had nodded, wide-eyed and eager to please, a habit ingrained in me since childhood—ready to be molded by someone wiser, sharper, someone who could see the potential in me I hadn't yet discovered. In a place like this, favoritism was everything, and Nikki's approval meant I was on the right track.

Her strange affection for me puzzled others as much as it did me. I wasn't like the others—the Eastern European girls with their busty figures, heavy tans, and unapologetic attitudes. They were loud, confident, and ruthless, swarming around the men like a pack of wolves, leaving no scraps behind. But I was different— more natural, more understated. My voice had an eloquence that men didn't expect in a place like this, and my softer approach appealed to those who sought more than just skin-deep lust.

It was probably that quietness that made Nikki pull me aside one night as I stood at my station fixing my makeup. She caught sight of the pink Agent Provocateur bag I'd set down by the mirror, a remnant of yet another shopping spree on Bond Street. Spending had become second nature—if I wanted it, I got it. Nothing was off-limits anymore. Whatever I bought, I'd make back in the evening. It was a vicious, exhilarating cycle.

"Heather," Nikki said, adjusting my garter and tucking a loose strand of hair behind my ear, "save as much as you can. This doesn't last forever." Her gesture was oddly maternal, the closest thing to care you'd find in a place like this. She wasn't wrong, but the new lacy black underwear was an investment, not just in my appearance, but in my success. In this world, you had to spend money to make money.

"Now get out onto the floor," Nikki said, her tone shifting to command. "Important customers tonight, far-right corner." I grabbed my small leather black purse and strode out the side door, determined to reach the corner before anyone else as my heels clicked against the floor. For me, the stakes felt high, and these customers Nikki was tipping me off about could mean the difference between a good night and a great one.

The club had its own hierarchy, a set of unspoken rules enforced by the cutthroat competition among the girls. I had learned them by watching the others work their craft. They'd push, shove, and charm their way to clients, hungry for attention and money. It was a hunt every night, and the men were the prey. But tonight felt different. As I approached the far-right corner, I noticed the men being seated. They were well-dressed, each cufflink and polished shoe exuding entitlement, that they were used to getting what they wanted, yet something was off. Their movements were too calculated, their eyes darting around the room like they were looking for something or someone.

I hovered near enough to catch their attention but far enough to maintain a touch of mystery. The key was always in the subtlety—being available but not desperate. As I adjusted my stockings, I strained to catch pieces of their conversation. They weren't the typical crowd of lonely businessmen or stag parties. These men had chosen this club for its discretion—a shield, I thought, for whatever illicit business they were involved in. "…the shipment needs to be…" "…he's getting impatient…" Their words were vague but laced with tension. This wasn't just a night of fun. It was a transaction where deals were sealed with a handshake under the guise of pleasure. I sipped my drink, smiling lightly, knowing I was witnessing something far bigger than myself, yet forbidden to understand fully.

One of the men, older than the rest with salt-and-pepper hair and a face etched with hard lines, glanced in my direction. Our gazes met for a brief moment, and I saw something within his eyes as he glared back. It wasn't desire or even curiosity—it was the kind of measuring look you give a weapon before deciding whether to use it. I was being assessed, weighed, judged for some unknown purpose. I gave him a wink, one I had perfected over countless nights, the kind that could pull thousands from a man's pocket. But inside, my mind was trying to comprehend what was happening. What had Nikki gotten me into? And more importantly, how was I going to navigate this situation safely?

As I took a step toward their table, purse in hand and secrets hidden behind my eyes, I could feel myself stepping into the real underworld. The game had shifted, and I was no longer just playing for tips and private dances. Now, I was playing for keeps. The men fell silent as I approached, and the older one leaned back in his chair, a slow smirk creeping across his face. His East London accent cut through the thick of the club as he said, "Well, well. What do we have here?"

I swallowed hard, forcing my smile to stay in place. "Good evening, gentlemen. I'm Heather. Can I interest you in some company tonight?" The words came out easily, a rehearsed line that had served me well in the past. But never had they felt so loaded, so fraught with potential consequences.

The man chuckled, a sound devoid of any real humor. "Heather, is it? Tell me, Heather, how good are you at keeping secrets?"

I hesitated, just for a split second, before responding with another practiced smile.

"Discretion is my middle name," I replied with a lightness that belied the growing tension inside me. "What happens with me stays with me."

He patted the seat next to him. "Sit down, love. We could use a pretty face at our table." I slid into the seat, careful to maintain my poise. The other men at the table regarded me with a mixture of suspicion and interest. He leaned in closer, lowering his voice. "Now, Heather, just smile and nod if anyone looks our way. Can you do that for us?"

I nodded, pouting my lips all while trying to compose my racing heart. "Of course. I'm very good at being seen and not heard."

His smile was cold, predatory. "Good girl. There's a nice bonus in it for you if you keep playing along."

Their conversation resumed, and I maintained my role as the silent, pretty distraction, sipping my drink slowly while trying to piece together their coded words. "…shipments coming in next week…" "…this won't be a problem anymore…" I wondered what—or who—had been "taken care of." But I laughed softly, as though one of them had told a joke, the mask never slipping. The older man glanced at me approvingly before continuing. I found myself thinking of Nikki, wondering if she knew exactly what she was getting me into. Did she have connections to these men? Was the club more than just a front for harmless adult entertainment?

Hours passed like a blur. Eventually, the older man pressed an envelope into my hand, his grip lingering just a little too long. "Here's a little something for your trouble." His voice was low and discreet.

I nodded, barely managing a polite thank you as they stood to leave. From across the room, Nikki caught my eye and gave me a nod, her expression unreadable, a silent acknowledgment of something bigger than just another night at the club. Back in the dressing room, the harsh fluorescent lights stripped away the allure of the club, leaving only exhaustion and questions.

Later, when I went to the manager's office to cash in, I found Derek already waiting for me, uncharacteristically focused on me instead of ignoring me as usual.

"Well?" he asked as soon as I closed the door behind me. "How was your night?"

I hesitated for a moment before sinking into the chair across from him, processing each thought as my chips rolled onto the table. Before I had a chance to answer, he sighed heavily, running the stack of crisp pound notes through the counting machine.

"It's complicated, love, and sometimes that means playing both sides." His eyes met mine. "You've done well, Heather. This is a good night for you, so I advise you to forget everything you heard." His words settled over me like a gentle warning, a reminder that in this world, silence was often worth more than curiosity.

As I left the club that night, the weight of the envelope in my purse felt heavier than it should. I hadn't opened it, but I didn't need to. It was thick enough to know that walking home wasn't an option. I slid into the back of the cab, its engine rumbling beneath me as the driver pulled away from the curb, carrying me into the night. The city smeared past in the rear-view mirror, lights reflecting off rain-slicked streets, as if nothing had ever happened. Inside me, the night still crackled like live wire. Leaning back against the seat, I exhaled slowly and made a silent promise to myself that I would use every skill I had honed, every lesson life had taught me to navigate this thing we call life, and not only survive but thrive.

I had come so far from that scared little girl in Ireland, the one who had once felt like an outsider in her own home, though in many ways, I was still her—still searching for my place in the world, still trying to understand the complexity of human nature. Familiar streets passed by outside the window, but they seemed different now, with London's towering skylines holding just as many secrets as I did.

As the cab rolled to a stop outside my building—a towering ex-council flat building in central London—I glanced up at the rows of windows, each one glowing faintly in the night. Every window represented a life, a story, its own world tucked away within the brick and mortar. I often wondered about the people behind those windows—their joys, their aches, the quiet routines. Were they like me, moving through life playing roles they hadn't chosen? Or did they feel grounded, certain of their place in this demanding city?

Looking up at the building, I was reminded of just how vast the world really was. Each window, a small piece of an enormous puzzle, made me feel both insignificant and connected at once. It was strange how a simple block of flats, with its worn facade and plain architecture, could hold such a multitude of lives. Staring up, I felt that familiar mix of awe and humility. The city felt endless, full of stories I'd never know but could feel the significance of all around me.

And here I was, just one story among thousands, trying to navigate my own path while the rest of the world spun on, unaware of the battles I fought behind closed doors. In moments like these, I was reminded of how small we all are in the grand scheme of things, yet how much power we hold within our own lives. Whatever life threw at me, I knew I could face it head-on. After all, that's what survivors do.

And if there's one thing I've always been, it's a survivor.

Looking back on this chapter of my life, I am struck by the complexities of human behavior as we navigate the pursuit of survival, connection, and self-preservation and the delicate balance between who we are and who we allow the world to see. Nikki's words resonate deeply with me: *"Give them a taste of what they think they want, but always keep a part of yourself hidden."* What began as pragmatic advice for the club now feels like a broader philosophy for life. There's a wisdom in keeping parts of yourself untouched, in safeguarding the pieces of you that no one else gets to mold or manipulate. Not out of fear, but out of self-respect. Real power isn't about control over others—it's knowing yourself beyond what anyone expects. It's preserving something sacred within yourself that no one can take away.

My night at the far-right table, laughing, feeling the vulnerability of my position among dangerous men, brought back brutal memories of the night the man had touched me without permission—his hand on my skin, an intrusion that still lingers in my memory. Time stretched unnaturally, the room tightening around me as I fought the urge to pull away. I had to smile through it, mask the discomfort, and continue playing my role, because that's what the environment demanded. But inside, I was shaken for a long time. That violation reminded me how easily boundaries could be crossed, how vulnerable I could feel, even in moments that might seem insignificant to the outside world. The moment was over in seconds, but the feeling stretched on, seeping into my bones, a violation so subtle it could have been brushed off by someone who had never known what it was like to live in a body that the world felt entitled to.

I started to question the trust I placed in men, the silent agreements I assumed were in place to respect my autonomy. I had believed, perhaps naively, that respect wouldn't need to be stated aloud. But if someone could so easily cross a line without hesitation, then what was to stop others from doing the same? That night shattered my illusions and taught me something more profound than just the vulnerability of my body—it exposed the vulnerability of my self-worth. The confidence I once had seemed to waver in the aftermath. I began to wonder if the power I held was real, or if it was only an illusion, something that could be stripped away just as easily as the layers of my clothing. With every unwanted touch came the slow erosion of the boundaries I had worked so hard to protect.

In that instance, I understood Nikki's advice in a new light. It wasn't just about preserving some mystery for the clients; it was about holding on to the parts of myself that no one had the right to touch—physically or emotionally. Each time someone tried to take more from me than I was willing to give, I reminded myself that I still had the power to protect what was mine: my soul, my identity, my worth. That was where my strength lay now, in consciously guarding the parts of myself that are sacred.

Most of us have parts of ourselves we keep just for us. It might be a secret dream, a private thought, or even a small ritual no one else knows about. These things don't always look like "boundaries" from the outside, but they're the quiet ways we stay connected to who we are.

Psychologically, this speaks to a deeper human need for autonomy. We all assume different roles throughout our lives, whether it's as entertainers, lovers, daughters, or employees, and in each of these roles, we are expected to give something of ourselves. We shape-shift, adapting to expectations, molding ourselves to fit the spaces we occupy. But the key to survival, I've learned, is to hold back enough to maintain a sense of self. In a world where others try to lay claim to pieces of your soul, that untouched part becomes your anchor, the compass that keeps you from drifting too far from who you really are.

The club was a place where power and control met vulnerability and humility. Men would come seeking fantasies, but beneath their desires was something deeper—a need for control. Control over their lives, over their circumstances, and in some twisted way, over us. I've often wondered how much of myself I am willing to give, and how much of me is defined by societal expectations. However, in these moments of doubt, I am reminded that my power lies not in submission, but in understanding the game of life for what it is and choosing how to engage. Real power isn't about dominance; it's about understanding the rules and deciding when to break them.

Spiritually, this experience has forced me to confront the duality of existence—the constant tension between light and dark, innocence and experience, power and surrender. Whether it be the men who enter the club or dating in modern-day society, we are not just seeking pleasure; we are seeking escape. And in that search for escape, we expose the most fragile parts of ourselves that are raw, broken, and hidden from the outside world. In vulnerability, I find my strength. The roles we play are not just about fantasy; they are mirrors reflecting the deepest desires and fears of those around us. And if you look closely enough, they will show you your own.

Life is full of such moments—when we must choose between performance and authenticity. It's easy to lose oneself in the role, to forget where the mask ends and the soul begins. But now, as I step into the woman I've become, I am reminded that survival is not just about enduring. It's about growing, evolving, and becoming more attuned to the world within me and around me. I am no longer the wide-eyed girl from Ireland, eager to please and desperate to be chosen. I no longer seek validation in the eyes of others or measure my value by how much I can give. I am a woman who knows her power, who understands the strength in discernment, in choosing carefully where and to whom she gives her energy to, and who values the part of herself that remains unreachable by the world's demands. Because in the end, survival is not just about playing the game better. It's about knowing when to step away from the table entirely.

CHAPTER 12

RED RED WINE

The world outside the club's velvet curtains should have felt different—less staged, more real—but in many ways, it was just another performance. I struggled to relate to men in the real world, in the places where I wasn't wearing five-inch heels or draped in sequins. Something inside me had shifted, and the rules that once seemed so clear—about what was real and what was fantasy—blurred until I couldn't tell which version of me I was supposed to be. I had spent so long protecting myself behind a facade of confidence and allure, curating a version of myself that men wanted, that when it came to meeting men in my personal life, I couldn't tell if I was still performing—or if I could trust them with my vulnerability.

James was a prime example of this paradox. He reappeared in my life unexpectedly, striding into the club one night with the same easy confidence I remembered, a small blue Tiffany box clutched in his hand. I hadn't seen him in a while—not since he had dropped off the radar after our meeting in the restaurant without a word—and I didn't expect to see him again. But there he was, standing in the dim light of the VIP area, his face lit up in a way that made it clear he thought he was about to sweep me off my feet. He handed me the box with a flourish, as if it was some grand gesture, some olive branch that could erase all the time that had passed. The box itself was tiny, deceptively innocent in its packaging, but it carried weight. Tiffany's. The brand alone was meant to signal something, to tell me that he was serious, that he wanted me. But what exactly did he want? I hesitated to lift the lid, wary of what lay inside—not just within the box, but within the claim itself.

He asked me out again, his voice smooth and sure, like nothing had changed between us. By opening the box, I made a choice. Nestled inside was a sparkling diamond necklace, its brilliance reflecting at me like a silent agreement. I didn't know why I accepted it. Maybe part of me still craved the fantasy he represented—a life where a man would shower me with gifts, treat me to fine dining, whisk me away to luxurious destinations. It was a story I had told myself for so long, the idea that I could be taken care of, that material gestures could fill the void that danced between my desire for independence and my longing for connection. Still, I let him take me to dinners before my night shifts, playing the part of the perfect companion, allowing myself to slip into the role he wanted me to play. But the truth was, I didn't trust him. I didn't trust any man, not anymore.

The game didn't end when I walked out of the club; it bled into every interaction, every glance across a crowded room, every whispered promise over a candlelit dinner. It lingered in the way I moved through the world, the way I assessed every conversation, every touch, every lasting look with quiet calcula-tion. I had spent so long deciphering what men wanted from me that I wasn't sure I knew what I wanted from them. Was this just another transaction? Was I giving away pieces of myself in exchange for attention, for gifts, for a sense of being desired? The line had blurred beyond recognition, and somewhere along the way, I had become fluent in a language I wasn't sure I ever meant to learn—the art of desire, of withholding just enough to keep them reaching, of playing a role so well that sometimes, I even forgot what was a performance and what was real.

At the same time, there was Harry. We met on Tinder, which, to me, already felt like a place where the game was rigged, where everyone was trying to sell themselves in the best possible light, hoping that someone would swipe right and validate their worth. But Harry was different, or at least he seemed to be. From the start, he pursued me with a kind of steady, old-fashioned determination, like something out of a romance novel but rarely seen in real life. He wasn't flashy like James, but there was something genuine about him, something patient and grounded. He was a gentleman—English through and through, with roots in the Surrey countryside. His background in finance at Deloitte gave him an air of sophistication, but it wasn't the kind that demanded attention. He was stable, structured, clean in every sense of the word. He made me feel like I could let my guard down, even though I was still wary of men, still unsure if I could trust anyone outside of the fantasy world I had built for myself.

For weeks, I kept him at a distance, letting him chase me because I wasn't ready to let him in. I wasn't sure if I was ready to let anyone in. But eventually, I caved. He took me out on a series of dates, and with each one, I felt a little more of the walls I had built around myself start to soften. By our fourth date, he whisked me away to Greece, a gesture so romantic and spontaneous that it took me by surprise. As I stared out at the Aegean blue sea with his hands wrapped around my waist from behind, I found myself wondering if maybe, just maybe, there was a chance for something real outside of the club, outside of the version of myself I had been performing for so long.

Meanwhile, James had planned a surprise trip to Prague. It was almost comical, having two men vying for my attention, planning trips across Europe like I was some kind of prize. It was the opposite of the world I was used to inside the club, where women competed for the attention of men, hustling and clawing for every bit of validation and money they could get. Now, here I was, with two men unknowingly competing for me, offering me glimpses of different lives, different futures, different versions of me. It was surreal, this sudden flip of power dynamics. I had always been the one trying to hold on to control, trying to make sure that I was the one who decided when and how I gave myself to someone. But now, the roles had reversed, and it left me feeling untethered. I wasn't sure if I liked it. I wasn't sure if I wanted it.

With Harry, things felt different—genuine in a way I hadn't allowed myself to believe in for a long time. There was an ease between us, a softness that made me forget, if only for a little while, the guarded version of myself I had learned to carry. I found myself looking forward to our dates, to the way he spoke to me like I was just a girl, not a mystery to unravel or a temptation to chase. He saw me as someone untouched by the shadows of the world I lived in, someone simpler, lighter, unburdened. To him, I was innocent, untainted by the complexities I had come to know too well. And for a moment, I let myself exist in that version of me—the one he saw, the one I wasn't sure had truly existed but wanted, desperately, to believe in.

But then there was James. He was giving me what I thought I wanted—the lavish gifts, the expensive trips, the bouquets of roses that arrived at work with an almost alarming regularity. He was generous in all the ways I had once believed mattered. Yet, something was missing. The night I finally gave in and slept with him in Prague, I felt like I had betrayed myself. The act, which should have meant something, felt hollow, transactional, like I had given away a part of myself in exchange for something that no longer held value. Lying next to him in the hotel bed, I swore to myself that night that I would never again give in to a man just to get something in return.

Something had changed inside me, and it wasn't just about James. It was about the club, about the life I had built, about the choices I had made. I started to resent going to work at night. I resented the way it made me feel, the way it chipped away at me, piece after piece, until there was nothing left but the act. I started seeking refuge in Harry's presence, wanting to be with someone who made me feel like I was more than the sum of my parts, more than the performance I had been giving for so long.

I tried to compress my shifts into one or two nights a week, pushing myself to make as much money as possible in short, intense bursts so I could take the rest of the week off to be with Harry. For a while, I felt like I was managing—balancing two lives, slipping between them like they were two separate realities. But it wasn't sustainable, and I knew it couldn't last. I was being pulled in opposite directions; caught between the world I had built and the one I was beginning to crave. The more time I spent with him, the more I felt the pressure of my life I wanted to leave behind. I needed an exit, a way to untangle myself from the dual existence I had been living.

In a bid to change my work environment, I auditioned for one of the most exclusive gentlemen's clubs in London. It was a different world altogether. The rules were strict—no cash in hand, no cheap tricks or hustling required. The clients were high-profile, the kind of men who didn't need to be convinced to spend money. The money was good, but the environment was cold, clinical. The club had a strict shift rotation, which meant I had no choice but to show up. It was worth it for the money, but it came at the cost of my freedom that I had once clung to so fiercely.

But despite the outward appearance of change, the reality was that people still wanted something from me, and I found myself feeling more trapped than ever. I was making more money than I had ever made before, but the cost was isolation. The other dancers eyed me with suspicion, their jealousy palpable. I made no friends, asked no questions, and blurred as much as I could from my memory. It was just work, a means to an end. Yet, even in that cold, sterile environment, a few clients stood out—men I'll never forget, for better or worse.

There was the afternoon client, a man with a penchant for melancholy and the song "Red Red Wine." He'd waltz in just as the daylight started to fade, his presence a ritual of sorts. The DJ, on cue, would spin the track, and he'd sink into a corner booth, lost in his own world. Our interactions were as predictable as his routine—no dance requests, just the simple companionship of a conversation that never ventured beyond the surface. Sitting with him was a guaranteed £100–£200, a lifeline for his blues and a steady stream of income for me. It was a strange sort of relationship, marked by routine and unspoken understandings, but one that was surprisingly comforting in its predictability.

Even now, when "Red Red Wine" sneaks into the air in an unsuspecting café or slips onto the radio, the memories creep back. The chords become more than just background noise, pulling me through a portal into those shadowy afternoons. I can almost feel his presence, the low hum of routine filling the space between us, a delicate exchange held together by silence and expectation. It's strange how something so repetitive, so seemingly insignificant, can leave such an imprint. The song remains a tether to those quiet moments—a subtle, haunting reminder of the strange comfort I found in the predictable dance of his loneliness and my understanding.

Then there was Michael. Oh, Michael. Among the countless customers who had passed through the club, he was unforgettable. Michael had a way of making everyone feel like they were the center of his world, if only for a night. His reputation preceded him—lavish gifts, extraordinary nights, and an aura of indulgence that drew every woman's attention. He'd often pay for five dancers to join him in a private booth, and while we danced and partied, the room felt like an exclusive haven, reserved just for us. Being chosen to be one of his dancers was like winning a prize, a validation that came with a sense of specialness.

But behind the glamour, Michael was more than just a generous patron; he became a kind of surrogate father figure in the chaos of the club. There was something comforting in his presence, as if being near him offered a momentary reprieve from the endless cycle of performance. He'd often invite me to his terrace house in Chelsea, a grand space that felt worlds away from the club's seediness and dirty secrets. His family resided in their country estate in Devon, and his Chelsea residence was like a secret retreat, a place where we'd sit with glasses of wine, and he'd spin tales of his escapades—sex parties, strip clubs, and glimpses of a life that always seemed larger than reality.

Michael wasn't one for subtlety. After a particularly slow night at the club, I casually mentioned that I could use some extra money, half-joking, half-serious, expecting maybe a bit of advice or a kind word. Instead, he invited me over to his terrace house in Chelsea for the first time.

The invitation was unexpected, catching me off guard. It wasn't some grand gesture; there was no intrigue or mystery surrounding it. Just a simple offer: "Come by, we'll have some wine, and I'll take care of you." He said it with the same ease as someone offering a lift home, as if this was just something he did—invite people into his world, if only temporarily.

At first, I hesitated. I wasn't sure what to expect, unsure if this was crossing a line I wouldn't be able to uncross or where the night would lead. But the need for extra cash dulled my reservations, and curiosity—always my greatest weakness—pushed me forward. Practicality won out in the end, and I found myself standing outside his grand Chelsea home. The kind of house that didn't just whisper wealth but announced it, filled with an eclectic mix of antiques and modern art, the kind better suited for a museum than someone's living room. As we sat there, sipping wine, the initial tension eased, replaced by the familiar rhythm of our conversations. His stories flowed effortlessly—decadent nights at exclusive sex parties, affairs that seemed pulled from novels, memories that painted him as both the hero and the rogue.

I listened, captivated, yet always aware of the fine line between the real and the performed. His wealth, which I had never fully understood, seemed boundless, but what struck me was his desire for company, to fill the emptiness with something meaningful, even if just for a few hours. All I know is that beneath the layers of wealth and spectacle, Michael was just another person searching for something real, something meaningful, and, perhaps, something to break the monotony of a life that, for all its excess, still felt incomplete.

CHAPTER 13

SHAME AND SELF-DISCOVERY

After a few months at the new club, life outside of work started to change in ways I hadn't anticipated. I began to see Harry more seriously as our relationship deepened. At first, it was easy to compartmentalize—keeping my nights at the club separate from our weekend dates, where the world of lap dances and curtained VIP rooms belonged to a different reality. But the deeper our relationship got, the heavier the emotional burden of my secrecy became and the harder it was to keep the truth from him. My schedule at the club made it difficult to juggle both worlds, and I could feel the pressure mounting like a ticking time bomb I couldn't defuse. Every conversation where I dodged his questions or gave vague answers about my employment pulled me further into the tension of living a double life. Harry's curiosity about my source of income and how I spent my time grew stronger, and the heaviness of that deception became unbearable. I knew that soon, I'd have no choice but to be honest with him, even though I feared what the truth might do to us.

Eventually, the moment arrived, and it came sooner than I was prepared for. We were at a café one morning, engaged in a seemingly mundane conversation about future plans, his work, and our upcoming getaway. It was in that ordinary moment that should have felt safe, I realized I couldn't build a future with him unless I was fully transparent. Harry needed to know what I did for work—no more vague answers or evasive maneuvering. Before I could second-guess myself or back out, the words slipped out.

"I work as a stripper."

The atmosphere shifted instantly, and I watched Harry's face as he processed the revelation. His expression was frozen, a mixture of shock and confusion. "A stripper?" His voice was tight, betraying more than just surprise.

The silence was dense, almost unbearable. My heart sank as I saw his eyes cloud over with hesitation. I knew this conversation would change things between us—how could it not? The burden of my confession lingered between us, and in that silence, I realized that as much as I tried to build a life outside of the club, the shadow of my double life followed me everywhere. No matter how much I yearned to escape the game, to live a life unburdened by performances and secrets, the stage was always waiting—and even if I were to walk away from the stage, it would always form part of my story. My past would always remain.

Even now, I feel it—the quiet pull of the past, the weight of its permanence. No matter how much distance I put between myself and that world, it remains, like a song I once knew by heart or a place I could find my way back to with my eyes closed. In moments when the future feels uncertain, when scarcity whispers its familiar threats, there's a part of me that knows the strip club is always there, waiting like an old habit, like muscle memory I could fall back into without a thought. No matter how much I wish to rewrite certain chapters, they remain a part of who I am. Each part of me—my past selves, my shifting identities, even that inner child who still longs for safety—unfolds gradually as I move forward. Those experiences, for better or worse, have shaped me, layering depth, resilience, and understanding onto the person I've become. My past may be unchangeable, but I see now that it is not something to escape. It is something to integrate, to honor, to allow as part of the story that is still being written.

As Harry sat there, lost in thought, I could feel the enormity of my truth pulling us further apart. His silence hung heavy between us, louder than any words. Then, without warning, he stood up, his chair scraping against the floor as he walked out of the café. Part of me understood why he walked away. Another part wanted to scream that this was who I was, and I deserved to be seen anyway. I sat there for a moment, stunned, watching the door swing shut behind him. The noise of the street outside seemed distant as I found myself left with nothing but the rawness of what had just happened.

Leaving my untouched coffee behind in the café, I wandered onto the streets of London Bridge, the city heaving as always, though I felt invisible, as if I were simply passing through. The truth I had buried for so long had cracked open, and now, in the light of day, I was forced to confront it for what it really was—unavoidable, undeniable. It wasn't just the truth about my job that weighed on me; it was the shame that clung to me like a shadow. Shame about my past, about the choices I had made, and how they shaped my sense of self. It was the shame of a childhood marked by instability, of a body that felt both exposed and unseen, and of a history I couldn't rewrite.

Carrying that shame affected me mentally, emotionally, and even physically. It burrowed into my body, embedding itself in places I didn't even know it could reach. It showed up as the tension in my shoulders, the tightness in my chest, and the heaviness in my breath, all physical manifestations of the emotional burden I carried. It lived beneath my skin, a silent undercurrent that dictated my every move. Some days, it whispered self-doubt; other days, it roared through me as defensiveness, quick reactions, or the need to control. It fed my anxiety, made me guarded, or shut down entirely—a fight response to a fear I couldn't always name, the brain's way of keeping me safe even when the danger was mostly in my mind. I had become so accustomed to its grip that I barely noticed it anymore, but it was there, quietly shaping how I moved through the world. Shame had built invisible walls around me for years. I didn't even know I was the one holding the bricks in place.

The chapter was closing, but it didn't feel like an ending—it felt like the emergence of something new, something deeply uncertain. What was left when the ego's relentless pursuit of validation and security was no longer driving me? Without the constraints of that job, freed from the judgments that had shaped me and the burden of accumulated shame, what is the true essence of my soul?

Still burning from the pain of Harry walking away without a word, I resolved to redirect my life. I pulled out my phone and started searching for a part-time job that felt safe, something I could actually show up to without dread. I didn't have all the answers, but I was determined to find a new path forward, to make something happen, no matter how it came about. I thought about the girls I had seen night after night at the club, many of whom would eventually disappear, leaving their old lives behind to begin something new. Their departures were a reminder that reinvention was possible, even if the details of their new lives were unknown to me. Their exits proved the possibility of escaping and starting anew, a concept that resonated deeply with my own desire for change.

I was also reminded of my mother's struggle after her split from my brothers' father—the Irishman who had never been able to accept me—or her, in the end. I watched her navigate the wreckage of her life as she not only faced losing her job, but also her husband and our stability. It was an entire upheaval of my life, an emotional and psychological battlefield. I remember vividly the rows of empty wine bottles that lined the kitchen counters and the floor of our childhood garden like ghosts. Her alcoholism consumed her, leaving her with a choice: to either confront her demons and rebuild what was left or to spiral further into the destruction that had already claimed so much of her life.

Despite these challenges, she chose to fight and managed to restore our lives from the ground up. Her strength and ability to start over has always been a source of inspiration for me. Witnessing her recovery from such devastation taught me that if she could heal from her lowest point, then I too possessed the ability to create a new life for myself. Reflecting on her journey in those raw hours after Harry walked away, I saw a mirror of my own path. Her capability to rise from the ruins of her former life was a powerful reminder that change, though daunting, is within reach for all of us. That real strength isn't just in enduring the worst of life but in choosing to rise from it.

In the years that followed working in the club, I began to sense that perhaps this was the real work: uncovering the soul beneath all the layers of identity I had constructed, the ones shaped by survival, expectation, and the need to belong. Beneath it all, who was I before the world told me who to be? That question became my compass, though I had no idea where it would lead.

Years later, deep in the stillness of an ayahuasca ceremony, seated across from a shaman in the flickering glow of candlelight, I finally found my answer I had been searching for all along. The freedom I had been so long chasing wasn't waiting for me in another city, another career, another version of myself. It wasn't something I could earn, buy, or seduce into existence. It was already there, in the quiet spaces between all the noise, in those moments where I stopped trying to be anything at all and simply allowed my soul to exist.

But before I could find those answers, I had to confront the reality of rebuilding my life from the ground up. There was no roadmap, no predetermined path to follow—only the knowing that I could no longer stay where I had been. Reinventing myself wasn't about chasing someone else's version of success; it was about taking deliberate steps toward crafting a life that felt genuinely my own. I knew I needed stability, something that gave me purpose beyond mere survival alone.

I ended up finding a part-time job that offered safety and purpose. In exploring my interests, I discovered a deep passion for fitness, which became a pivotal part of my journey. I'd always enjoyed exercising and going for long runs, but engaging in fitness at a new level and embracing that passion not only helped me regain confidence in my body but also provided a renewed sense of strength and self. Each class, each lift, each small milestone left me feeling a little lighter, a little more in control of my life. This process of self-discovery and change wasn't straightforward. It was a series of small, uncertain decisions, each one a step away from my past and toward an unknown future. Although I didn't have a clear vision of where I was heading, I knew that retreating to my old life was not an option. I recognized that if I could rescue myself once, I had the inner power to do it again.

I look back now and see myself grappling with the raw question of my own essence. Who was I beyond the personas and roles I had built and hidden behind for so long? What remained when the illusions were stripped away, when the identities that once served as my protection were removed? In moments of self-reflection, I find myself reconnecting with a part of me that had long been buried—the inner child, the little girl who yearned for safety, love, and a sense of worth. She was a tender, vulnerable, craving reassurance, affection, and to be valued for who she truly was. I remember her, with her wide, hopeful eyes and the silent dreams she held close to her heart. She wanted to be cherished, to know that she mattered, and to discover her place in a life that sometimes seemed overwhelming and dangerous.

As I peel away the layers of my adult self, I am drawn back to this little girl who still exists within me. She represents a part of my past that is deeply intertwined with my present, a part that has shaped my desires and fears that have guided my choices. Reflecting on her, I realize that much of my journey has been about finding ways to take care of and nurture her. The roles and personas I constructed were, in many ways, a means of protecting this inner child from the harsh realities and uncertainties of life. They were disguises that I wore to create a sense of control and manage the fears and insecurities stemming from my early experiences—perhaps more than I ever acknowledged.

Now, as I confront the core of my being, I am also addressing the needs and desires of this inner child. I am learning to offer her the love and safety she always sought, to feel her pain, and to provide her with the validation and comfort she needed. It is a process of reconciling with the parts of myself that were neglected or overlooked. By reconnecting with this inner child, I aim to heal old wounds that were overlooked, to fulfill the dreams she held, and to create a sense of self that is not only resilient but also knows that I am enough as I am.

If there's one thing I've learned, it's that healing isn't a straight path you can sprint down. It's slow, messy, and full of unexpected turns. The layers of who I am—my past, my identities, and that inner child who just wanted to feel safe—keep unfolding, revealing themselves as I move forward. But I've come to accept that. Healing is a process that requires patience, self-compassion, and a commitment to living in truth. As I continue to evolve and grow into the woman I am, I'm reminding myself—and maybe you too—that this journey is about trust. Trust that, little by little, you are healing from the past and the wounds that, in some way, may have always been there to shape you into the person you're meant to be.

CHAPTER 14
METAMORPHOSIS OF A DANCER

In early 2017, the twinkling lights of the club faded into the sterile glow of a high-end Kensington gym. My enthusiasm for fitness and self-care had led me to a part-time job as a nameless receptionist during the day, and it felt as though I had stepped out of one world and into another entirely—an abrupt, jarring transition from the seductive environment of nightlife to the clinical, disciplined atmosphere of daytime fitness. The contrast was confronting to my ego: from commanding thousands per night to counting down hours for a mere £8 an hour, this shift forced me to confront the ego's quiet whispers about worth and success. Paradoxically, this mundane existence felt like a lifeline to normalcy in my life, whatever that was.

Each day, I sat behind the sleek reception desk, observing the parade of sculpted bodies and designer clothes, feeling both admiration and a pang of longing. At night, the intoxicating energy of the club still called to me. Once or twice a week, I found myself drawn back to the stage that was the only place that felt like home, albeit an ill-fitting one. This bittersweet ritual of returning to the club was both a comfort and a reminder of a world I was trying to leave behind.

The human mind is indeed a maze of contradictions. Exhilaration can coexist with exhaustion, and the body's pleasures with the soul's quiet cravings. This duality forced deep reflection. On one hand, I was pursuing a simpler, more disciplined life at the gym, while on the other, I still felt the pull of the high-energy strip scene. In this great paradox, we chase dreams of wealth, status, and freedom, only to find they come with hidden costs. Time slips away, friendships wither, and our moral compasses spin wildly. The conflict within my choices was a psychological battleground where my inner desires clashed with external realities. This existential crisis, I've come to realize, isn't unique to ex-dancers or twenty-somethings. It's the universal human condition—a cycle of death and rebirth we move through over and over again in our lives. Holding on to past versions of ourselves hinders our ability to create the new space needed for growth. For me, the challenge was not just letting go but understanding who I was in this new context. The gym, with its focus on self-improvement, became a sanctuary where I could invest in myself rather than pour my energy into others.

Ironically, the constant engagement with strangers, once a source of adrenaline, became an unexpected drain on my vitality. I had spent years perfecting the art of social interaction, of reading people's desires and mirroring them back, but nobody had ever taught me how to recharge from it all. Nobody had told me that true self-care wasn't just about tending to the body but about nurturing my soul. It took time to learn that rest involved listening to the whispers of my inner self, knowing when to retreat, to be still without guilt, and to trust in the unfolding of my journey. There's a fine line between ambition and self-destruction, between striving for success and succumbing to societal conditioning that equates rest with weakness. My relentless pursuit of more money had come at a significant personal cost, and I have learned the hard way never to sacrifice more than I am willing to lose.

Amid these reflections and the routine of my gym job, I found a new outlet for expression: social media. As I sought ways to channel my passion for fitness and self-improvement, I began documenting my journey online. Initially, I was indifferent to the world of social media, but the growing interest that people showed in my fitness journey quickly drew me in. Reflecting on how I went from someone eager to remain invisible in the club to someone laying bare every detail of my life online—my meals, training routines, and daily rituals—it felt as though my past self was wryly laughing at this newfound transparency.

People latched onto my journey with surprising intensity that I hadn't anticipated. Whether it was perfect timing or a sprinkle of luck, my small account grew rapidly. The girl who once counted bills in the backroom of a club was now counting followers and likes, the immediate feedback of social media mirroring the instant gratification of applause I had once thrived on. Navigating social media, I drew on skills honed during my nights in the club. The art of captivating an audience, mastered on the dance floor, translated well to crafting engaging posts. Just as I had learned to read a room and gauge the energy of the crowd, I now attuned myself to the highs and lows of online engagement. The resilience I built, dealing with difficult customers and long nights, helped me face the occasional negativity that came with increased visibility. I developed a thick skin, learning to differentiate between constructive criticism and baseless judgment. This discernment became invaluable as my follower count grew and diverse opinions flooded my comments section.

Still, there were moments when I felt like an impostor in every role I played—too "sophisticated" for the club scene, not polished enough for the high-end gym clientele, and not quite authentic enough for my growing online audience. It felt as if I was caught between worlds, belonging to nowhere and everywhere all at once. Then, one afternoon at the gym, while I was organizing membership forms behind the desk, I noticed a familiar face approaching. It was a regular customer from the club. My stomach churned with unease, bracing for an encounter that could expose my past. I had always feared that being recognized would force me to confront my insecurities, whether I liked it or not.

To my surprise, the man greeted me with a warm smile and said, "I know you've reinvented yourself, but you haven't lost your spark." His words were a gentle reminder that the true source of shame often comes from cognitive patterns within rather than from others. In that moment, I realized that the judgment I feared was more a reflection of my own self-doubt than of external scrutiny. His recognition and kindness offered a profound lesson in humility: that despite our attempts to compartmentalize our lives, there's a shared humanity in all of us that transcends our roles and past mistakes. It was a small but powerful affirmation that maybe my past didn't have to define me.

Despite the growing confidence I projected online, I remained deeply uncomfortable with that chapter of my life. The thought of my followers discovering my history as a dancer filled me with dread. What if they judged me? What if they saw me differently? The fear of losing the respect and admiration I had worked so hard to gain was overwhelming. So, I did what felt safest. I made a conscious decision to keep my past hidden, carefully curating my online presence with precision, showing only the versions of myself that felt acceptable, admirable, and easy to digest. I convinced myself it was necessary, that it was just a small omission, but in reality, I was splitting myself in two again—who I was and who I wanted the world to see.

I became adept at sharing posts that were authentic in their way—documenting my fitness journey, my struggles with self-discipline, my wins from bodybuilding competitions—but always stopping short of revealing the full truth of my experiences and past. This division wasn't ideal, but it felt necessary. I told myself that perhaps, someday, I would find the courage to fully integrate all aspects of my identity. For now, as my follower count grew and opportunities began to open up, I chose to keep my past in the shadows, focusing instead on the future I was striving to build.

Even now, I find myself compartmentalizing my experiences, attempting to keep my past self at arm's length from my present. However, in doing so, I deny a crucial part of who I was and am, which creates cognitive dissonance. Learning to integrate both my past and present selves has been a journey of healing, helping me understand how each moment wove into the next chapter of my life. The confidence and body awareness I developed as a dancer now informs my approach to fitness, while the resilience built in the club helps me navigate the challenges of building an online presence. My experiences working in the gym as a trainer added depth to my understanding of human behavior and motivation. My identity is and always will be complex and often contradictory. While outwardly I present a confident, empowered image to the world, internally I am still on a journey of self-acceptance, learning to embrace all parts of myself even those I once kept hidden from the world until now.

As my social media following began to grow, the excitement of exploring this new phase of my life took center stage. The passion I felt for immersing myself in a world where I was both safe and in control became my motivation for a new life. Slowly, almost unconsciously, I found myself easing out of the nightlife scene, not with a grand farewell or a dramatic exit, but through a quiet, unspoken transition. It was only in hindsight that I realized my last night in the club had been, in fact, my final performance.

Reflecting on that final night, I wish I had known it would be my last time leaving the stage. If I had, I might have approached it with a different mindset, savoring the moment rather than treating it as just another shift. Maybe I could have looked with more gratitude around the dimly lit room that felt like home, acknowledging the endings taking place before a new beginning. Maybe I would have honored the determination it took to exist in that world, the strength it took to walk away. But instead, it slipped by almost unnoticed, a casual goodbye lost in the rhythm of routine, another shift I barely registered or remember. I was so absorbed in my transition to a new chapter that the significance of that night escaped me until I had already left my past behind.

Had I realized that this seemingly never-ending job would one day in fact end, I would've done many things differently during my entire time working as a stripper. For one, I would have paid closer attention to the stories of the people I met. Each interaction, each person who walked through those doors, was a fragment of a larger mystery that told the story of human connection and vulnerability. I would have taken more time to listen and show more of who I truly was, rather than just performing a role. I also would have invested more in myself, both emotionally and financially. The money came fast, and it disappeared just as quickly. Financial education was something I hadn't received—like many of us—and as a result, I often spent impulsively rather than saving and investing wisely.

I remember Nikki's stern look and wise words about saving money. The immediate gratification and glamour of nightlife meant money was spent recklessly. I was often caught up in the rush of cash flowing in and out, blissfully ignoring the financial wisdom she was trying to impart. I thought little of the future, believing that the present would always be abundant. In hindsight, despite leaving the club with very little to my name, Nikki's advice was a gift in disguise—one I was too young, too reckless to fully appreciate. It may not have felt like it at the time, but walking away from the club with very little to my name was a harsh but necessary lesson. It was that financial instability that forced me to reconsider my priorities and eventually reshaped my approach to life.

What working as a stripper provided me was far more valuable than any immediate material gain. It gave me the opportunity to start anew, to build a life that reflected my true self and aspirations. I remember the pride I felt when I first moved into my own apartment in London—a space I had created entirely for myself. It was more than just four walls and a place to live; it was proof of my independence, a symbol of everything I had fought for. I meticulously chose my furniture, selected fancy bed linen that made me feel like a queen, and purchased clothes that made me feel a deep sense of pride and self-respect. Each item was a physical reminder of the progress I had made, a reflection of my autonomy and the new chapter I was writing for myself.

This unconventional life also gave me something priceless—the freedom to travel on my own terms. For the first time, I was able to step into the world without hesitation, wandering through the romantic streets of Paris, basking under the golden sun in Ibiza, tracing history through the winding alleys of Eastern Europe. But these trips were more than just vacations; they were about losing and finding myself, standing alone in a crowd and feeling the exhilarating realization that I was completely free. Each adventure peeled back another layer, teaching me how to be alone without being lonely, how to exist without the need for external validation.

Beyond travel, this period of my life allowed me to build something from the ground up, to create without the immediate pressure of a conventional full-time job dictating my every move. I immersed myself in fitness, videography, and the creative pursuits that lit me up. It was a time of raw self-discovery, of uncovering what truly mattered to me and redefining success on my own terms. I no longer felt tethered to societal norms and dictated by financial necessity; instead, I was free to follow my passions and create a life that was one I had always dreamed of.

So, despite the mistakes and regrets that are part of my past, I see how everything worked out in its own way. The journey from the club to my current life here in Bali was not a linear path but a complex yet beautiful story with lessons and growth. Each misstep, each moment of doubt, contributed to the life I have today. I have learned to appreciate the ebb and flow of my experiences, understanding that even the most challenging times have led to profound growth and invaluable insights, which I call a "blesson." Every phase of my life, no matter how different or disconnected it seemed at the time, is a crucial part of my identity.

As we navigate this ever-evolving path, we must learn to do so with gratitude. Each one of us has an entirely unique story. Although my journey has not followed a conventional trajectory, it has led me to a place of genuine fulfillment and self-awareness through learning to surrender and look inward. I am learning to embrace the contradictions, celebrate the progress, and learn through the challenges. Through it all, I remain committed to living authentically, pursuing my passions, and continually growing into the person I aspire to be.

CHAPTER 15
THE BUTTERFLY EFFECT

The butterfly effect teaches us that even the smallest actions can ripple outward, shaping our lives in ways we often can't foresee. During those months working at the fitness center and leaving the club life behind, I was navigating my own growth and transformation, unaware of how my past was quietly intertwining with my present, or how my life was shifting beneath the surface. They say you should pause to appreciate the beauty around you, but it's often only in hindsight that you realize what you had. Lost in the whirlwind of daily life, I failed to recognize the profound changes taking place right before my eyes.

Social media was completely new to me. I didn't know trends or strategies; I was just trying to figure out how it worked. It was simply an outlet where my creativity could roam free, and for the first time, I felt a genuine sense of belonging. One ordinary day, as I manned the desk at the gym, a pivotal moment arrived. I logged into my social media account to pass the time, responding to comments, when I noticed one of my videos had gone viral overnight. My followers jumped into the thousands, then tens of thousands with every refresh. Soon, brands and PR agencies were sending messages, wanting to work with me. One moment, I was a receptionist, quietly piecing together a new life. The next, I was the center of a whole new world. This wasn't part of my plan, or even something I'd aspired to. It simply happened, from one day to the next. But sometimes, life has a way of surprising us.

In some ways, I'm grateful that I ventured into this new domain driven by wonder rather than strategically crafted marketing plans. The spontaneity of it all, the sheer thrill of discovery, gave me an authentic experience that felt organic. Still, I often ponder how far I might have gone with proper support and guidance from the start. Nevertheless, this journey taught me a profound truth: Embracing the unknown and seizing opportunities can unlock extraordinary possibilities. Whether it was the alignment of fate, the power of persistence, or an element of chance, what emerged was a serendipitous gift—an opportunity I hadn't even known I was seeking. This revelation speaks to a deeper spiritual and psychological awareness that when we open ourselves to the mysteries of existence and allow ourselves to be guided by our authentic desires, we often find the universe or something greater conspiring in our favor, revealing pathways we never imagined.

Without even realizing it, I tucked my dance bag—stuffed with heels and fishnet stockings—into the back of my wardrobe, unaware that I would never take it out again or that my heels would never again see the stage. In its place, I turned my focus toward building my social media presence, unaware that this shift would mark a pivotal moment: I'd never return to the dance floor. My lunch breaks became impromptu filming sessions for my workout videos, and weekends turned into a chance to vlog my life. Every moment was an opportunity to capture the world around me and document it on social media.

I couldn't believe it when invitations started arriving for PR events with global brands. Soon, boxes of products showed up every day—luxury skincare, stylish activewear. This world was something I had never aspired to; in fact, I hadn't even known it was possible. But soon, I found myself jetting off to Paris with Disney and soaking up the sun on idyllic islands with Discover Greece. I had become the aspiration for many, an example of the possibility of fame.

Then came the day a talent manager named Danny from a prominent influencer agency met me in a nearby café on my lunch break. His presence was magnetic, and as he spoke, I felt a spark of courage within me. He encouraged me to take the leap—to quit my job at the gym and go all-in on social media. "Trust me," he said, his eyes steady and sincere. "If you commit to this, the brand deals will follow, and opportunities will flood in."

I had built my new life around the security of a steady paycheck, yet here was a chance that felt akin to the hustle of the club but promised something more significant. I envisioned the projects I could pursue, the connections I would make, and the life I could create—unbound by the confines of my previous routine and work schedule. As I made the decision to hand in my notice that very day, surrendering my security for the promise of something greater, I felt the weight of my past begin to lift. Yet, amid the excitement, a lingering doubt remained: Would I truly find purpose in this new reality? Would things really work out for me?

This wasn't just about going viral or stepping into a world of influencers and brand deals. This was about the courage to redefine myself. To trust that my life wasn't a series of disjointed chapters, but rather a fluid, ever-evolving narrative—one where every experience, no matter how distant or unrelated, was intricately connected to the next. It was all leading me somewhere, but like a butterfly, I knew that in order to truly fly, I'd have to surrender to the wind, even if I didn't know where it would take me.

The universe is strange. Somehow, it gives you exactly what you need at the precise moment you need it. But I knew that to fully receive those gifts, I had to let go of the version of myself that was clinging to safety. I had to let go of the girl who found security in routines, in familiarity, who found solace in predictability. I had to let go of the dancer—the woman who had once believed her worth was in the way she moved, in the way she made others feel.

Harry and I moved into a modern high-rise apartment, its glass walls making it feel as if we were floating above London. Yes, he had walked away after I told him I was a stripper—but not for long. He came back, and we slipped into our routines again, relating to each other as though that conversation had never taken place. In our new apartment, the view was everything I had dreamed of—an endless sweep of city lights, bridges, and towers that felt like they belonged to me, to us. We converted the second bedroom into a content studio, a bright white room with impeccable lighting, always waiting for me to step in front of the camera. It felt like I was building a new stage, but this time, instead of hiding in the shadows, I was in the spotlight. Just like the club, I was on display, but I was trying to be seen in a way that felt more controlled, more deliberate.

Days were like a blur of excitement and opportunity, with brand deals from global names rolling in, and red-carpet events where I rubbed shoulders with the very influencers and celebrities I had only ever admired from a distance. There I was, standing beside people I had never truly seen as just other humans navigating the world, and yet, they were no different from me. We had all mastered the art of illusion, shaping our lives to carefully reveal only the qualities that made us appealing to our audience. Though, the qualities that made me appealing as an influencer were different from those that had made me successful as a dancer. It wasn't unlike the life I once led in the club. Still, there were significant differences. For example, as I wandered the streets of London, instead of trying to blend in or hide parts of myself, I wanted to be seen. I walked those streets as if I owned them, camera in hand, capturing snippets of my life to share with the world. Each post was a performance, each story a new chapter in the persona I was shaping.

But even though I was no longer living the club life Harry had nearly walked away from, there was still a dissonance between this new life I was building as an influencer and the life Harry lived. He was the quintessential London office worker: crisp shirts, early mornings, quiet dinners after long days of meetings. His routine was structured, predictable, and comforting in its way. He supported me, or at least he tried to, but I could feel it— the unease that simmered beneath the surface. His disapproval of my old life in the club that we never fully spoke about was now replaced with a silent tension about my social media presence.

It was as though the more visible I became, the more distant he grew. I could sense it in the little things—the way his smile faltered when I talked about a new collaboration, or how he seemed disconnected when I was filming, his quiet footsteps fading into the background as I focused on the camera. He would say he was proud of me, but the words felt hollow, like he was supposed to say them rather than something he truly felt. It was in the way his hand lingered in his pockets instead of reaching for mine, the way he seemed to shrink whenever I stepped further into myself. I wanted to believe he meant it, that he was cheering me on, but I knew he was trying to convince himself more than me.

Deep down, I never felt like I was truly enough for him. I was standing just outside the edges of his world, a world where money and security had smoothed out life's sharp edges, cushioning him from the kind of hardships that had shaped me. His parents were always polite, always gracious, but beneath their well-meaning small talk, I could sense their unspoken judgment. I was something unfamiliar, someone they couldn't quite place, a question mark in a world where reputations were carefully guarded. And Harry, for all his kindness and generosity, never truly grasped that part of me either. How could he? He had never known the feeling of being backed into a corner with no safety net, of navigating a world that never handed out second chances. He loved the parts of me that were easy to love—my ambition, my charm, the way I could hold a room in the palm of my hand. But the rest? The nights spent dancing under neon lights, the primal fight to survive, the fire inside me that came from learning to stand on my own—those were the parts he would never truly grasp. Not because he didn't want to, but because our worlds were never built to align.

We fought to hold on, clinging to familiarity more than to each other. The life we had built together looked beautiful on the surface, but beneath it, cracks were forming. I could feel the tension stretching tighter with each passing day, like something was bound to give. There was comfort in the routine we had created—in the quiet moments of watching TV after dinner, in the shared bed that had become more of a safe haven than a place of intimacy. The truth was, I was becoming someone even more distant from the version of me Harry had struggled to accept from the start. He had never liked me working in the club, and now, as my social media presence exploded, I was diving headfirst into yet another new world he didn't understand. My life was becoming more unpredictable and unconventional, far from the stability he valued. Though he tried to be supportive, with each brand deal, trip abroad, and every post that laid my life bare to a growing audience of strangers, he pulled further away.

We weren't ready to face the truth yet, as I continued to build my world online, neither of us was willing to admit that the life we had built wasn't enough to keep us together anymore. It was as if my life had split in two once again—one foot in the glamorous, chaotic world of social media and fame, the other in the structured life I thought I always wanted with Harry. But the harder I tried, the more unbalanced everything became. I couldn't ignore the growing distance, the small silences that felt louder than any argument. I couldn't ignore the feeling that maybe, just maybe, this life I had created for myself, no matter how shiny and perfect it looked on the outside, wasn't quite as fulfilling as I had hoped.

Just like in the club, I was performing again, only now the stage was different. And once again, I had to wonder—was this really me, or was it just another role I was playing, hoping to be seen, hoping to be enough.

CHAPTER 16

FOLLOW YOUR SOUL

You could never count on the same man coming back twice in the club, just as you couldn't count on the same brand offering to renew a contract or expect the same success on a post or video going viral. It was the gamble of being your own business and the sole architect of your success but also the sole bearer of its uncertainty. Over the years, this constant instability began to take its toll, especially with the rise of social media and the ever-increasing pressure to stay relevant. Maintaining interest with fresh content wasn't good enough anymore; it was about looking perfect—having visible abs, staying thin, keeping up with the illusion of an enviable life. My success was inextricably tied to my appearance, and every pound gained or tiny imperfection that broke through the facade became ammunition for strangers to tear apart.

For every loving and devoted follower who encouraged me to keep showing up, to keep being authentic, there seemed to be a hundred others lurking in the shadows, ready to criticize every detail. What had once felt like a space of connection and possibility was slowly becoming a toxic arena of judgment, one I was ill-prepared to navigate. Social media no longer uplifted me—it suffocated me.

The thick skin I developed for handling the insults of drunk men at the club became the same armor I had to wear online. In the club, slurred insults and degrading names were thrown my way to make me feel small, to exert some imaginary dominance in an environment where power was constantly shifting. I had learned to detach, to brush off their comments with a practiced indifference, but the truth is, some things stick. Even now, I can recall the exact words of their cruelty, as though they had buried themselves in places where my own insecurities already lived. There's something deeply imprinting about people coming for your looks, your character, the core of who you are. Over time, I had taught myself to recognize these words for what they were—a reflection of someone else's internal misery, their distorted view of the world projected outward. But that didn't make them any less painful or easy to carry.

The reality was, despite the happy character I presented online, after the initial high of my social media success, I had become deeply unhappy. Harry and I were at a crucial point in our relationship. As we packed up our London flat to move into our first home in the Surrey countryside, I felt myself unraveling. I felt disconnected—not just from him, but from myself. Years of restrictive dieting had left my hormones in chaos, my emotions numb. It was as though I was a ghost in my own life, going through the motions but not truly living. I was lost again, in a way that felt terrifyingly familiar.

As Harry packed up the flat around me, preparing for the next chapter in what should have been our happily-ever-after,

I remained frozen. I was physically there, but mentally, I was somewhere else entirely. My life was moving forward, but I was stuck, desperately clinging to the identity I'd forged online and the identity Harry and I had formed as a couple even as both slipped through my fingers. Every day, the house grew emptier as Harry carried boxes one by one to our new home. I couldn't face the life that awaited me because, deep down, I knew I didn't want it. I didn't know how to communicate with myself, let alone with Harry, but my intuition was screaming at me. This wasn't my path.

I sat in the hollowed-out shell of what had once been our home, scrolling endlessly through listings for one-bedroom apartments I could afford. London was expensive, too expensive, and part of me was searching for any excuse to escape. Not just from Harry, or the flat, but from everything I knew. I was moments away from sending an inquiry for an overpriced flat in a city I didn't even like when my phone rang. It was my mum. It was as though she knew. Without thinking, I answered. And as I heard her voice on the other end of the line, something within me cracked wide open.

"Mum," I whispered, staring at the email I was about to send. "I don't think I can do this."

"Why would you stay there, Jade, when you could go anywhere in the world?" she asked, her voice steady but full of warmth.

She was right. I hadn't even thought of it that way. Suddenly, it was as though a spark had been lit inside me, one I hadn't realized I was waiting for. Why limit myself to a cramped flat in a city I didn't love when the world was full of possibilities? I opened my laptop and typed "Bali" into the search bar. Months ago, I had saved a picture of Bali to my phone—an image that had been tucked away, forgotten, buried deep in my camera roll.

But now, it felt like a manifestation, like the universe had been waiting for me to notice. Within an hour, I'd booked a flight. It was as impulsive as it was freeing.

For the first time in months, the fear of my future began to lift. I dove headfirst into planning—accommodations, visa application, the works. But there was still one thing left to do: I had to tell Harry. I had to tell him that I was leaving for Bali—for two months, maybe more.

"I need to do this for me," I whispered, tears streaming down my face. Harry paced back and forth, his eyes wide with confusion and hurt, trying to wrap his head around what I was saying.

"How are you going to take care of yourself?" he blurted, his voice sharp with frustration.

The words landed like a slap. In that moment, it felt like time stopped. His question lingered between us, and just like that, everything became crystal clear. Harry didn't think I could take care of myself. After everything I'd been through, after every battle I'd fought and won, he still didn't see me. Not really. He didn't see the strength I'd summoned to pull myself out of the darkest places, the resilience that lived in my bones, the way I had built myself up again and again with nothing but sheer determination. Maybe his words came from a place of love, from a misguided need to protect me, but they landed like doubt, like disappointment. As we stood there in the middle of our half-packed life, holding each other through the tears, I knew this was the end, maybe not forever, but at least for now. Some endings arrive with slamming doors and shattered glass, but ours arrived in the quiet, in the knowing, in the realization that love is not always enough.

Days later, I packed my life into a suitcase, piece by piece, as if careful folding could soften the finality of it. Each item tucked away felt like a quiet goodbye to the life I thought I wanted. Harry drove me to the airport in silence, the hum of the engine the only sound between us. It felt surreal, the quiet knowing in my bones that everything was about to change. But I had no idea how much.

"It's only two months," I said, trying to breach the deep divide that had formed between us. "And then we'll move into the new house."

Harry's face remained impassive. And then, as we pulled up to the terminal, he finally spoke. "Goodbye." That was all. No reassurance, no promises, no last-minute confessions. Just a single word. His voice was flat, distant, as though he had already accepted the finality of our relationship. I swallowed against the lump in my throat as I stepped out of the car, my suitcase rolling behind me. As I fought back the tears and made my way through security, I felt as if I was leaving behind more than just a relationship. I was leaving behind a version of myself—a version I was finally ready to let go of.

A final boarding call for my first connecting flight through China echoed through the terminal as I boarded the plane and found my seat. I took a deep breath. This was it. My suitcase held everything I thought I needed, but what I truly needed couldn't be packed. I needed to find myself again. The plane began to taxi, and as it lifted off the ground, I felt a strange sense of release as I relaxed back into my chair. I didn't know what was waiting for me on the other side, but I knew it was time to rediscover who I was and to let go of the parts of myself that no longer fit.

The first few days in Bali brought a flood of emotions. The air was thick and heavy with humidity, wrapping around me like a second skin. The roar of loud motorbikes echoed in the streets, creating a chaotic yet soothing backdrop to my solitude. For the first time in years, I was truly alone. No obligations, no familiar faces, no one expecting anything of me. It wasn't just freeing—it was unsettling. In the evenings, I would take my journal and sit in tiny cafés, sipping herbal tea, surrounded by people I didn't know, speaking a language I barely understood. I had never felt so small, so invisible.

Loneliness crept in during those quiet evenings. I'd watch couples laugh together, groups of friends sharing stories, and families wandering the streets, all while I sat alone, an outsider looking in. My days were filled with the sensory overload of the bustling island, yet my nights were hollow, filled with the ache of being a stranger in a new place. It was a strange contrast: Bali's beauty was magical, but it also magnified the emptiness I felt inside.

Slowly, though, I began to adapt to my new life. I began trusting my body again, shedding the strict dieting routine that had consumed my life in London. I treated myself to meals that were wholesome and nourishing, not designed to fit a calorie count or a restrictive plan. I indulged in the exotic flavors of fresh tropical fruits, the delicate sweetness of handmade desserts, and vibrant dishes that made me feel alive in a way I hadn't felt in years during my fitness competition and social media career. Every meal was a small act of rebellion against the rigid control I had once imposed on my body and a significant act of love toward the person I was becoming.

I started taking myself out on what I called "solo dates" to restaurants, workout classes, and markets. I became my own best friend, my own biggest supporter, my own lover in the sense of learning to cherish myself. I was learning to enjoy my own company, to revel in the freedom of doing whatever I wanted, whenever I wanted, without anyone else's input. The nervousness I felt in the beginning, the discomfort of eating alone in a restaurant or wandering the streets without a companion, slowly began to dissolve. I realized I wasn't as lonely as I feared. In fact, I was discovering something deeper: the ability to be at peace with myself.

Bali had unfolded before me, revealing pieces of myself I had buried for years. The island wasn't just a place; it was a mirror, reflecting back the parts of me I had spent years neglecting. I wandered through sacred temples and along white sand beaches, but the real journey was inward into the hidden corners of my own mind, the spaces I had been too afraid to explore before. Here, time moved differently. There was no rush, no pressure, no expectations to be anyone other than who I was. I wasn't performing, wasn't proving, wasn't chasing anything other than presence itself. For the first time in a long time, I felt like I was enough.

I watched the sun dip below the horizon in Canggu, the sky painted in hues of gold and pink, reflecting the transformation within me. I felt an overwhelming sense of clarity; even though I'd only planned on being here a short time, leaving now would be premature. I had only begun to scratch the surface of who I truly was. My journey of healing through breathwork workshops, energy healing sessions, and confronting long-held traumas from childhood was just beginning. If I left now, I would be abandoning myself all over again. With a heavy heart, I knew I had to have a difficult conversation with Harry. Over the phone I shared the depth of my healing work, hoping he could understand why I wasn't ready to return. I hoped he would understand. I hoped, maybe, he had been doing his own inner work too. But when I asked if he had been reflecting on himself, if he had been processing the changes between us, his response was flat.

"No disrespect, but I have a lot less spiritual damage I need to work with."

His words cut deeply, exposing a disconnect that I could no longer ignore. I felt any remaining affection I had for him shatter. I took a deep breath and replied, "I just wanted to let you know that it's too soon for me to leave." My decision was clear, grounded in the realization that my journey was far from over.

"Well, what do you want me to say? You've made your choice." Harry shot back, a sharp edge in his tone. I felt the pain in his words, a reflection of the hurt and confusion that mirrored my own. Yet, even in his anguish, I knew that our paths had diverged. This was our ending—a painful, inevitable parting.

After our call, I took a long walk. Under the expansive, starlit sky, I felt a profound sense of peace. I was no longer the person who had left London, lost and fragmented. I was becoming someone new—someone who understood the importance of listening to her own heart and following the call of her soul. This chapter of my life had taught me the significance of honoring my journey, no matter how painful or uncertain. As I prepared to face the next stage of my life, I knew that my time in Bali had been a crucial step toward becoming the person I was meant to be. At the time, I had no idea that Bali would be a much larger chapter in my life, and that I would still be here, five years later.

CHAPTER 17

HALF THE WORLD AWAY

I hadn't given up entirely on social media, though I struggled to keep up the same content I had shared in London—those tightly scheduled days of shoot, edit, upload that once ran like clockwork. My life had shifted so dramatically that the posts I once shared effortlessly now felt out of sync with my new reality. The difference wasn't just the change in location; it was as if my internal world no longer matched the curated life I had portrayed online; what I lived and what I posted were two different things. I longed to uncover who I truly was beneath the surface-level sharing, but I didn't know how. I was still figuring out who I was, one unsure day at a time. There was an almost noticeable sense of disconnect between the version of myself that still existed online and the woman I was becoming. I'd open the app and feel a jolt. The vibrancy of my fitness posts, where every caption seemed filled with certainty, now felt alien. In Bali, my days were quieter and more introspective, and though I still felt the pull to share, I hesitated. What part of me was I supposed to show the world now? The carefully constructed fitness influencer persona no longer felt authentic, yet I wasn't quite ready to step into something new. I didn't have words for it yet. The in-between felt like an identity crisis unfolding in slow motion.

Despite my efforts to maintain the same online presence, part of me was desperate to rebel against my former self. If I wasn't that girl anymore, who was I? I found myself gravitating toward bars and one-night stands, seeking to reclaim the youthful experiences I felt I had missed or to simply grasp at a semblance of normality. I wanted to experience freedom without the constraints of being a fitness influencer. The late nights out and short-lived connections became an escape—moments where I didn't have to perform, diet, or be "on-brand" for anyone. Yet even in those small moments of rebellion, something felt off. The freedom I sought seemed just out of reach, slipping further through my fingers the harder I tried to hold it. Balancing the persona of a dedicated social media figure with that of a carefree twenty-four-year-old was proving to be an overwhelming challenge. The truth was, I wasn't sure if I wanted to be either anymore.

Social media, despite its inconsistencies, remained my main income, with a few digital products on the side—enough to scrape by, not enough to relax. However, the income wasn't reliable. Even though Bali wasn't as expensive to live in as London, and even though I was spending more judiciously than ever, I still questioned whether I could sustain my new life in Bali on social media income alone. There were moments where I would sit in front of my laptop, staring at the analytics, trying to force myself to care about follower counts and engagement metrics. But the numbers felt meaningless, just data on a screen that no longer represented me or the life I was actually living. The transition from the London media scene had been more difficult than anticipated, with partnerships dwindling and my lack of enthusiasm for social media becoming increasingly apparent. This blow to my confidence made me feel as though I wasn't good enough, further amplifying the weight of my doubts and insecurities. I started to wonder daily if I had made the right decision in coming to Bali. The vibrant, tropical paradise that had seemed like a place of freedom was now feeling like an island of uncertainty. Would I be able to build a life here? Or was this just another temporary escape, another chapter I would eventually leave behind?

Determined not to return to a life I'd outgrown, I threw myself into side jobs: admin work, social media management, personal training, whatever covered rent and groceries. Each role seemed to come to me serendipitously, as if the universe laid a stepping stone just as I was about to fall. Whenever I was on the brink of despair, someone from a past event or a mutual friend would reach out, offering me an opportunity, keeping me afloat just long enough to figure out my next move. It was as though Bali had its own rhythm, and despite the chaos within me, it was slowly guiding me toward something more solid. But that didn't make it easy. Some days were filled with doubts, others with small victories that kept me going. There were moments when I wondered if I should pack up and leave, head back to the familiar, but something kept me grounded in Bali. Perhaps it was the slow pace of life or the friends I had made that brought me back to myself, reminding me of the reason I had come here in the first place.

After months of uncertainty and countless attempts, a high-end gym I frequented offered me a permanent position. It was a turning point—a validation that my efforts were paying off. Just a week before receiving the job offer, I had made the internal decision to stay in Bali no matter what. My six-month visa was nearing expiration, and I applied for a new one: paperwork, passport photos, waiting rooms, steps toward putting down roots. I moved into a shared villa with two new friends, feeling a sense of belonging that had eluded me in London. The job at the gym felt like confirmation that I could build something real here, and with that job came a sense of routine and purpose in my life. Although I sometimes questioned whether I was going backward after working for myself and experiencing the highs of the club and the media, the ease of each day—knowing what lay ahead—brought me peace. In a way, Bali had made the decision for me. I was staying.

As I settled into my new life, everything began to fall into place. I had a stable job, a comfortable home, and for the first time in years, a group of real and dependable friends. These were all things I had desperately lacked in London, where most of my social connections felt superficial and tied to the endless scroll of the digital world. The sense of grounding and community I experienced in Bali was nothing like the life I had known before. The laughter shared over communal meals, the late-night conversations under the stars, and the support from my new friends felt profoundly different from the momentary interactions and isolation of my past life. I was starting to see that maybe this was what I had been searching for all along. Something deeper, more meaningful, and rooted in the present.

The pressure to maintain a social media presence began to slowly fade as I focused more on the genuine connections I was building offline. Still, part of me felt the loss of my online presence acutely and wanted to blame external factors—followers who no longer liked my posts, brands that had stopped reaching out. Even though the pressure was fading, and even though it wasn't something that felt like it fit me anymore, it was still a loss I had to grieve, and it hit me hard. My sense of worth had been so closely tied to external validation—likes, comments, sponsorship deals—and when that began to slip away, it shook the very core of my identity. Who was I without them?

During that time, I had to confront the uncomfortable truth that my sense of success had been built on the approval of others. Letting go of that was excruciating, forcing me to look inward for the validation I had spent years chasing externally. I could no longer find my worth in being deemed relevant by the digital world. I didn't want my sense of value to depend on anyone else's approval. Slowly, I began to realize that losing the version of me I had built online wasn't a failure. It was a necessary release, allowing me to step into a more authentic version of who I truly was. The island was teaching me the importance of listening to my own heart and following the call of my soul, and I was determined to continue honoring that truth, no matter where life took me next.

One day, on a whim, I signed up for a women's circle that promised connection, vulnerability, and a space to express the parts of myself I had kept hidden for so long. The intimate group session was a place to heal our inner child, reclaim our essence as women, and reconnect with our bodies. We danced around the room with our eyes closed, letting our bodies be swept away by the rhythmic sound of the drum, each beat echoing our collective heartbeat. The room felt alive with shared intention and quiet, unspoken understanding. In this sacred space, we began to lower our walls, sharing the reasons our souls had nudged us to gather, recounting stories of pain and truth that had long been buried beneath layers of silence.

These were stories that needed to be told, stories of resilience, of women supporting each other through unimaginable challenges, of the complex humanity that existed in a place often judged from the outside. As I listened to the voices around me, I felt a sense of purpose I hadn't experienced before. My purpose was no longer merely to survive or chase what came next—it was to embrace who I was now and let that guide me. I thought back to my years at the club. That life had changed me, yes, but it no longer had to be something I kept hidden. Instead, I could finally use my voice to share that story openly. I realized that in sharing our truths, we create connections that could support and empower every one of us.

Sitting in the circle, I allowed myself to openly talk about my past and the pain I had carried for so long, revealing the lost relationship with my father that I had yearned for, and the complete disconnect from my body that had haunted me. In that moment, I saw a reflection of all of us—the dancers, the clients, and myself. We were all searching for connection, for validation, for that fleeting moment of truly being seen.

Tears streamed down my face as I connected with that lost, lonely part of myself. For the first time, I felt a sense of wholeness, a coming home to myself that had eluded me for so long. True healing had begun. As I left the women's circle that evening, I felt like a new version of myself, a version that embraced vulnerability rather than shying away from it. I walked barefoot along the beach, the sun setting in the distance, dressing the sky with hues of colors that made me feel alive. Each step in the warm sand felt grounding, a reminder to appreciate life for everything it was, both the beauty and the messiness.

But as peaceful as it was, the healing journey was far from easy. I couldn't just snap my fingers and rid myself of the need for validation or make peace with my past overnight. There were days when doubt crept back in, insidious and familiar. I'd scroll through Instagram, seeing the lives of people I once compared myself to. Their curated lives and visible success still triggered that nagging feeling that maybe I wasn't doing enough. Maybe I was missing out on something essential. That's the dangerous thing about social media—it's like an old flame that keeps calling you back, even when you know it's not good for you, a seductive pull that can distract you from your own journey.

Despite these moments of weakness, I remained committed to my healing. I understood that I had to confront those parts of myself that still craved the approval of others, however uncomfortable that process felt. The more I dug into my past, the clearer the roots of my insecurities became. Growing up, I had always felt the sting of rejection from my father, a void that left me searching for worthiness in all the wrong places. In his absence, I had unwittingly replaced that need with external validation from the world. But Bali was revealing to me that this kind of validation was fleeting, and ultimately, meaningless.

As I kept attending workshops and healing sessions, I found myself drawn to different practices, each offering new insights into my past. One weekend, I attended my first ayahuasca retreat nestled in the jungle of north Bali. The experience was intense, profound, and nothing like I could have ever imagined. During the ceremony, emotions that had been buried deep within me resurfaced. I felt anger, grief, sadness—everything I had suppressed over the years surge upward. The female shaman guided us through the ceremony, reminding us to stay present through the discomfort. "You're getting well," she said. "It's messy, it's painful, but it's your responsibility to heal."

Her words struck something deep within me. In that moment, I realized how much of my life I had spent avoiding discomfort, numbing myself with distractions. I had filled every empty space with something—social media, one-night stands, surface-level friendships—anything to keep me from confronting the pain that was hidden deep within me. I had mistaken busyness, external validation for self-worth, and avoidance for true strength. But Bali was stripping all of that away. There was nowhere to hide here, no noise loud enough to drown out the whispers of my soul. The island, with all its beauty and stillness, was forcing me to face myself in a way I had never before. To sit with my emotions I had buried, to feel the discomfort instead of running for it, to surrender to the process of real healing. And in that surrender, I began to find my way back home to myself.

After the first of what turned out to be many ayahuasca retreats, I turned to journaling with a newfound devotion. Writing became a safe space where I could express the parts of myself I hadn't yet found the courage to share with the world. I wrote about my fears, my desires, and my dreams, pouring out my heart onto the page. I wrote about the woman I was becoming—someone who was free to be who she truly was and capable of manifesting the life she envisioned. And it wasn't just about letting go of the past; it was about embracing the present and the future with openness and curiosity. For the first time in as long as I could remember, I wasn't worried about what came next. I wasn't obsessing over my next career move or how many followers I had gained or lost. I was living in the moment, learning to trust that whatever path I was on was the right one.

The relationships I was building in Bali also played a huge role in my growth. I met people from all walks of life—fellow expats, locals, travelers from every corner of the globe—each with their own unique story and reason for being there. There was Jana, a breathwork facilitator from Germany, whose journey had brought her to Bali after years of corporate burnout. She invited me to her circles, where I began a deep internal journey to reclaim the inner child I had long buried. Jana had a grounded presence, her mousey brown hair always tied back in a loose bun, and her calming voice guided us through the sessions as we tapped into our breath to release old emotional patterns. There was a quiet wisdom in her, a deep understanding of the body's capacity to heal itself when given the space and attention.

During those sessions of deep, rhythmic breathing, I started to reconnect with parts of myself I had forgotten. Breathwork drew me inward, forcing me to face wounds from my past I had long kept hidden. Jana's gentle encouragement to surrender made me feel safe enough to explore those vulnerable spaces. We would sometimes talk after the sessions, sitting under the shade of palm trees, talking about the layers of life we were each unraveling. Her approach to healing was unlike anything I had known—intuitive, unforced, deeply attuned. It was exactly what I needed at that stage in my journey.

I also met Jero Mangku Geni, a Balinese healer—the word *Mangku* is a priestly honorific. He had spent his entire life in the same village. His presence was grounding. He spoke little, but when he did, his words were filled with wisdom that penetrated your soul. His eyes, dark and gentle, seemed to see through the layers we all wore to protect ourselves from the world. It was the Mangku who taught me that healing was not just about letting go of pain but about understanding it, integrating it, and allowing it to be part of who we are.

The connections I made felt genuine, free of the pretense that often accompanied networking in London. There were no ulterior motives, no hidden agendas. We were simply just humans, trying to figure out life together, sharing laughter and tears in equal measure. Each person I met was a mirror reflecting a part of myself back at me—whether it was Jana's ability to reinvent herself or the Mangku's profound acceptance of life's ebb and flow. It was these relationships, these raw, unfiltered moments of connection, that allowed me to open up in ways I hadn't before.

Bali had become a place of rebirth for me, where I truly embodied the power of self-love as I invested everything I had into my healing.

Some of my most profound experiences came through working with a woman named Shelly. With her guidance, I explored energy and somatic bodywork, diving deep into both the physical and emotional layers of healing. I had always been open-minded and curious about alternative approaches, so I was eager to embrace this journey. Something about Bali felt like the perfect place for this exploration, and I was ready to do anything that might bring me closer to my true self. Her sessions often took place in a quiet open-air room, where the hum of cicadas and the warm scent of burning sage became part of the rhythm of the work. As I lay on the mat beneath her, I could feel my body trembling, sometimes resisting, sometimes softening into her touch.

The sessions were painful yet transformative; I felt years of built-up tension and trauma release from my body. There were moments when tears and cries came without warning, as if memories stored deep in my muscles were finally finding a way out, and other times when a strange, vibrating stillness filled me, a silence I had never known before. It was as if I had been carrying the weight of the world on my shoulders, and for the first time, I was learning how to put it down, piece by piece.

CHAPTER 18
BROKEN OPEN

As I continued to heal, something beautiful happened: I began to feel a deep sense of gratitude. Gratitude not just for the beautiful moments, but for the journey I had been on, for the struggles that had led me here, and for the woman I had become. I began to enjoy the simplicity of life, the kind of joy that didn't require an audience. Mornings became sacred: a quiet coffee on the balcony, watching the sun rise over the rice fields. I spent hours by the ocean, letting the waves lull me into a state of calm. I walked barefoot in the sand, feeling the earth beneath my feet and grateful for every step that had brought me here. The pain, the doubt, the fear—all of it had a purpose after all. I saw that without each and every part of my story, I wouldn't be who I am today. Slowly, I began to embrace the imperfections, recognizing that they were part of my growth. What once felt like failure now just felt like life, shaping me into someone stronger and more real.

And then came love. Not the romantic whirlwind I had chased for so long, but a quieter, more enduring love—the love I found within myself. I started to see that I was already whole; I didn't need anyone else to complete me. The love I had been searching for externally had been inside me all along, waiting to be acknowledged. This self-love was different from the fleeting rush of validation I had once craved; it was steady, rooted in acceptance, and unwavering in its presence. For more than two years, I stayed completely single, dating no one. I almost forgot about dates and seeking romance entirely, as I began to romanticize my own life.

I poured all the energy I once gave others back into myself—learning, growing, healing. Life became a dance of self-celebration, where I found beauty in the smallest things, and became someone I fell in love with. I no longer needed anyone else to fill the space inside me, because for the first time, I had filled it myself.

Eventually, I tried to open my heart again. I thought I was ready, thought I had healed enough to let someone in. That's when I met Ryan. At first, he seemed like everything I had been waiting for: charming, attentive, full of passion. But as quickly as things blossomed, they began to decay. Slowly, every wound I thought had healed began to surface, raw and aching. His casual comments about seeing other women sparked jealousy and doubt within me. Then there were the nights he arrived late, stumbling through flimsy excuses and lies. I couldn't help but replay every previous betrayal in my mind, each memory a ghost haunting my present. Why did he always seem to choose the world over me?

Ryan brought up every insecurity I had worked so hard to bury. He played the hot-and-cold game, leaving me in constant states of confusion, triggering an anxious attachment and fear of being abandoned that made me cling tighter the more he pulled away. It felt unbearable, the kind of ache that made sleep impossible, my mind looping through his words until I could no longer tell if I was losing him or losing myself. I tried to rationalize his behavior, excusing red flags as passion, convincing myself that if I just understood him, if I just loved him more, he would commit to us.

He lied. He cheated. He slept with other women—one of them my best friend—while still looking me in the eyes and telling me he loved me. The betrayal cut deeper than just his actions; it was in the way he made me doubt everything about myself. I had done so much work on myself, invested so much in self-love and healing. How, after all that painstaking work, had I allowed myself to fall into this trap with someone? I kept trying to make sense of it all, twisting myself into knots as the old accusations crept back into my head: Maybe you're not enough. Maybe love would always mean pain. I thought if I gave him my whole heart, he might change. But he didn't. And with every lie, the stability I had fought so hard to build began to crumble. The confidence I had painstakingly rebuilt started to slip away, unraveling despite all I had done to protect it.

The rage came out in waves. I yelled out to God, punching my bed in frustration, soaking my shirt with tears. Each outburst was a release, a desperate attempt to purge myself of the pain that I felt inside my heart. What was I supposed to do with all this hurt? I sat alone in coffee shops, staring into nothing, trying to make sense of it all, while my heart ached with every breath. And yet, every morning, I put on a brave face and headed in to work as if nothing was wrong. I'd smile at people while my phone buzzed with texts from friends who had seen him out with other women the night before, when he had told me he was home working. All the while, my heart fractured under the weight of knowing someone I trusted had made a game of my love. I pretended everything was fine, because for a time, pretending was the only way I could survive.

I knew it was coming. It always did—like clockwork, every month. Ryan would push me away, shatter my world into pieces, and then, like a twisted boomerang, pull me back in with whispered promises of "I love you," and "I'm sorry." As I felt the familiar pattern begin again, I questioned why I was willing to endure it all once more. Why was it so hard to let go of something I knew was hurting me? But a time finally came when something was different. I wasn't sure if it was my healing or the exhaustion from the endless cycle, but I knew I couldn't do it anymore. The guilt of his actions had become too heavy even for him to get blackout drunk and ignore.

We were in a coffee shop, having our morning coffee. We sat there in silence, his eyes softer than usual, though I could see the storm behind them.

"Hey," he began quietly, as though he knew he was bringing bad news. His voice wavered slightly, making me wonder if he was second-guessing himself or if he just wanted to get it over and done with.

I didn't respond at first, just watched him. My heart didn't leap anymore when I saw him—it felt heavy, like it was carrying the weight of every broken promise, every lie I had tried to forgive.

"I—uh, I have something for you." He handed me a folded letter, avoiding my eyes entirely. "I…I thought this might help explain."

I didn't even need to open it to know what it said. I had heard it a hundred times before, in so many unspoken absences and halfhearted apologies. Still, I unfolded the paper, my fingers steady, heart bracing for the familiar sting. Was I ready for the confession hidden within those lines and lies?

"I want to thank you for everything," he began, his voice wavering. "You've been amazing to me. More than I deserve. But…I need to let you go. I need you to find your soulmate."

These were words that once would have gutted me, but now they only skimmed the surface.

The rest of the letter was the same blend of sweet words twisted with bitter truths. The usual mix of sentimentality and selfishness. He thanked me for everything. For "loving him through the chaos," he wrote, as though it had been a vague "chaos" that had hurt me and not his choices—his repeated lies and infidelity. He promised I would always have a place in his heart, but said that he needed to let me go. And there it was: the confirmation of what I'd known all along.

"Also, I should probably tell you…" he continued, and I could already hear the familiar twist coming. He had the decency to look shamefaced. "I've met someone else."

I didn't flinch. Rather than feeling sad or broken, something unexpected happened. I felt sorry for her. Not in a condescending way, but with deep compassion, because I could see through him. I knew exactly how this would play out. She would feel the highs, the intoxicating love bombing, the way he first made her feel like the only girl in his world. And then, little by little, he would chip away at her self-worth, just as he had done to me. Those late nights, the unanswered texts, the gut-wrenching moments of doubt. And one day, she would stand where I stood now, reading a letter that was never meant to be sincere.

I looked at him, and for the first time, I didn't see him through the lens of love or longing. I didn't see the man who had destroyed me. I saw the boy he once was—the brokenness he carried from repeating cycles he had never dared to break, the scars that had shaped him. I had compassion, not for his actions, but for the circumstances that had made him who he was. But I also understood something far deeper now: We all have the ability to change, to make better choices, as I had.

His suffering didn't absolve him, and his brokenness wasn't a justification for the damage he inflicted. It was a conscious choice to destroy his life and anyone who came close enough to care. He knew what he was doing, yet he still chose to keep hurting those around him. That's when I realized his poor treatment of me for so long had absolutely nothing to do with me. His betrayal wasn't a reflection of my worth; it was a reflection of his inability to love himself. He was a man drowning in his own self-destruction, pulling anyone close enough to care into the undertow with him.

"I hope she can see who you really are," I said, and though the words were meant to hurt, I meant it, truly. For her sake, I wanted her to avoid the same games I endured. "I don't want her to feel the pain I felt because of you."

"I'm sorry," he whispered.

Bitterness surged in my heart at this apology that meant nothing.

"What? You're sorry you fell in love with someone else?" I cut him off. "How could you do this to me, Ryan?"

He ran a hand through his hair, frustration evident on his face. "It's not that simple. I was lost.… I didn't want to lose you, but—"

"But you did," I interrupted, tears welling up. "You made your choice."

For the first time in a long while, I walked away and never looked back.

I was broken once more. But this time, it wasn't the same kind of brokenness I had known before. I was broken open. The pain was unbearable, but in its rawness, it also revealed truths I hadn't been able to see. From the shattered pieces of my heart, I realized that I had let someone into my life who mirrored the old version of me—the one who sought validation in all the wrong places, the one who believed she wasn't worthy unless someone else said she was. He wasn't letting me go. I was already gone.

Ryan's betrayal was a devastating reflection of the fact that, despite the long path of healing I'd already traversed, there was still a long path ahead. As much as I had loved myself during those two years I'd spent alone, without romantic entanglements, there was still a part of me that didn't believe I deserved real love. With Ryan, I had accepted far less than I was worth. And through all the lies, all the heartbreak, I learned that love should not bring that level of suffering with it.

Love doesn't make you question your worth.

Real love is steady. It doesn't toy with your heart or diminish your sense of self. It doesn't force you into self-doubt or leave you bending over backward to prove you're enough. Love isn't a game where you win someone's affection by enduring their cruelty. It's about mutual respect, trust, and kindness. Love builds you up, creating safety and security, rather than chaos and confusion.

For too long, I thought love meant sacrifice—giving all of myself, even if it left me feeling empty. But now I see that love doesn't drain you; it fills you. Love is not about how much pain you can endure for another person; it's about how much joy, peace, and growth you can share together. Real love doesn't leave you feeling broken; it heals. It doesn't push your boundaries or make you feel less than; it honors who you are and grows alongside you.

In recognizing the importance of masculine and feminine polarity, I realized that true connection flows from a place of balance. The masculine embodies strength, protection, and stability;

the feminine brings nurturing, intuition, and emotional depth. In a healthy relationship, both energies harmonize, creating a dance of support and love. Real love allows both partners to embody their true selves without fear or compromise, embracing each other's strengths and vulnerabilities.

I finally understood that love isn't something you chase or have to prove yourself worthy of. It's something you attract when you truly know your self-worth. Love flows into your life when you stop settling for anything less than what you genuinely deserve. I poured so much energy into relationships, not realizing they were reflections of the relationship I had with myself. When I didn't value or respect myself, I attracted people who mirrored that back to me. As I grew in self-love, my standards shifted. I no longer tolerate mistreatment or settle for less than I deserve. My boundaries became clearer, not as walls to keep people out, but as guidelines for how I want to be treated—with kindness, respect, and honesty.

Eventually, in the aftermath of Ryan, the need to prove myself to anyone faded away. I no longer felt the urge to announce my achievements or broadcast my healing journey for validation. My worth wasn't tied to what others thought of me, and that realization was perhaps the greatest gift of all. I had finally come home to myself. Ryan's presence in my life had been a test—a brutal, heart-wrenching lesson in love. But from that pain, I awakened to a deeper truth. I learned that real love begins and ends within me, rooted firmly in self-acceptance and respect. I realized that I would never again allow someone to diminish my worth or make me feel less than whole.

Just as I was reclaiming my strength and finally letting go of Ryan, life threw another curveball. I lost my job of four years at the gym—a place that had been my constant through all the chaos. It felt like the ground beneath me had shifted again, leaving me unsure of how I'd move forward. I had no idea how I would support myself, how I would manage to stay in Bali without a job, or how I'd figure out my visa situation. It felt as if every layer of security I had clung to was being stripped away.

In that moment of uncertainty, something shifted within me. Instead of sinking into fear or panic, I found a strange sense of calm within. The universe had been nudging me toward something greater, and though I couldn't yet define what that "something" was, I trusted that this wasn't the end but rather a new beginning. I had faith in myself, in the strength I had built, and in the belief that everything would somehow work out. The fear that used to paralyze me was replaced with confidence. I didn't have all the answers, but I no longer needed to. I was learning to let go of control and trust that, no matter what, I would find my way.

CHAPTER 19
MIND, SOUL, AND MEDICINE

It had been a while since I stood at the edge of a decision, yet here I was again, facing the inevitable truth: It was time to rewrite my story once more. I was again faced with the realization that I could either remain face down in the gutter of suffering or reach toward the stars and what was infinitely possible. It was in that space between what was and what could be that the questions began to rise, persistent and unrelenting. Where was life guiding me? What was the purpose in the pain? Why am I even here, and what for? Was I just a small fragment in an indifferent universe, or was there something more waiting for me to discover?

These questions lingered within me, urging me forward as I couldn't ignore the pull of something beyond the physical. Life wasn't just asking me to endure—it was calling me to explore, to question, to seek. So, I did. I embarked on a quest, one that took me to the doorsteps of mystics and into the embrace of ancient wisdom. It was a pilgrimage, not through deserts or mountains, but through the recesses of my own consciousness. Each moment felt like a revelation, peeling back layers of who I thought I was and revealing the essence of who I was meant to become.

I immersed myself in books, attended workshops, and sought out ceremonies. I found myself lost in the pages, fingers tracing words that sparked a fire within me. I began to find answers in the teachings of spiritual leaders, philosophers, and healers who understood that the physical world was just the surface of existence. They spoke of realms unseen, of energies and spirits, of universal truths that transcended human understanding. I sought their wisdom like a wanderer searching for water in the desert. I wasn't just looking for answers—I was looking for myself, for the parts of me that had been buried under years of societal conditioning, trauma, and fear.

I had once believed that healing was a destination, a place you arrived at once the wounds of the past had been mended. But I was wrong. Healing was a journey, a continuous spiral, each loop bringing me closer to a deeper truth. Every experience—whether painful or joyous—was a lesson, an opportunity to grow. The deeper I went, the more I understood that true healing wasn't about erasing the past; it was about integrating it, about recognizing that whatever I thought I knew was just the beginning. There was so much more beyond my conscious understanding, waiting to be uncovered when I was ready.

Perhaps it was my intuition or the guidance of my own soul that led me to seek out a ceremony with two shamans from Colombia who had come to Bali. Upon entering their sacred space, I sensed a profound shift within me. The air was thick with the aroma of burning herbs and the low hum of ceremonial songs, forming a fragrant veil between worlds. This wasn't my first plant medicine ceremony, yet there was something about the energy in this shala that told me I wouldn't walk out the same person I was when I entered. My skin tingled with anticipation, as though the universe itself was aligning to guide me further into my journey. This was a chance to pilgrimage deeper into myself, to connect with the wisdom of the plants and the ancient traditions that guided the shamans. The medicine they offered was a powerful ally in my quest for understanding, a gateway to insights that lay beyond the ordinary.

Gathered in the shala, the two shamans spoke of their calling to the plants, a calling that resonated deeply within me. They shared stories of their journeys—how whispers of nature and plant spirits had invited them into a world of healing. They spoke passionately about our collective responsibility in this sacred space, reminding us that we were not mere participants but active co-creators of our own healing. "The plants offer wisdom," one of the shamans said, "but the answers lie within you. Our role is to guide you back to the wisdom that has existed all along and surrounds you."

We all sat in a circle, a mixture of anticipation and vulnerability unconcealed among us. Each of us waited for our turn to step forward and drink the first cup of yagé, the Amazonian brew that had the potential to unlock doors within our souls. Flickering candlelight cast dancing shadows on the walls, softly reminding us of the light within, even as we prepared to plunge into the unknown. Then, as if on cue, the candles were blown out, plunging the space into darkness. Silence wrapped around us, inviting introspection as we settled. The first hour was filled with quiet contemplation, the only sound the gentle rustle of collective breathing. I closed my eyes, turning inward, feeling the medicine circulating through my body.

Drinking this medicine was unlike anything I had ever experienced before in a ceremony. The bitter taste lingered in my mouth as the liquid slid down my throat, but it wasn't just the flavor that unsettled me—it was the sudden shift in reality. It began as a gentle warmth, a soothing wave that rolled through me, coaxing out the tension I hadn't even realized I had been holding. As the yagé coursed through my veins, pulling me away from the confines of the dark room and into a realm of colors and patterns. Visions and shapes I could not name danced behind my closed eyelids, twisting into journeys that both hypnotized and terrified me. I felt as though I had entered a game of my own mind, each level unfolding with greater complexity and depth. Shapes morphed and melded, intertwining with buried memories, revealing secrets I had spent a lifetime trying to forget.

Boundaries between my mind and soul blurred, dissolving under the guidance of plant spirits whispering in my ear. I was both a witness to my deepest wounds and the healer soothing them. The experience wasn't just psychedelic—it was a raw, visceral confrontation with the truths embedded in my bones. I faced my subconscious, my ego, the layers of my mind playing out my fears right before me. As the night progressed, the visions grew more intense, more vivid. Shadows danced around me, evoking traumas that surged to the surface—some painful, others bittersweet. The visions were so overwhelming I felt as if my mind was tormenting itself, but the songs—those ancient, haunting melodies—reminded me that I was safe, that this was part of the process. The memories weren't there to harm me; they were there to reveal what needed healing.

There was no escape, only surrender. Once the journey had begun, there was no way of stopping it. Fragments of my past unfolded like scenes from a movie, each one inviting me to confront the emotions I had tucked away. In that moment, memories washed over me—of my mother's silent struggles, how I often sensed her pain late at night when I would hear her cries through the thin walls. Her pain felt like a dull ache—ever-present, lingering, even when I tried to ignore it. I had learned to put on a brave face, to hide my own fears, believing that my strength could shield her from the weight of her sorrow. Yet, deep down, I was just a little girl, feeling lost and confused, wanting to comfort her even as I tried to protect her from my own fragility. It was a subtle exchange, one where her tears silently revealed the scars of unseen wars.

The faces of women who had come before me flickered in and out of my consciousness—mothers, grandmothers, sisters—each one shaped by the heaviness of their stories. "I'm sorry," I whispered into the darkness, feeling their presence surrounding me. I wept for them, each tear healing not just me but the feminine itself. We are all interconnected, each of us holding our own burdens and triumphs, our wounds and wisdom. The weight of our shared history pressed against my chest, compelling me to acknowledge not only my own suffering but also the pain passed down through generations of women who had walked this earth before us.

As the hours ticked by, I was transported to moments of loss and heartache, feelings that had been buried under layers of distraction and denial. The medicine acted as a magnifying glass, illuminating the places within me that needed healing. It was as if I was inside my own veins, feeling the suffering moving through my body. I felt anger and sadness rippling through me, a relentless surge of tormenting emotions demanding to be felt. A torrent of emotion moved through me with the force of a storm, pushing me under, into the depths of my pain. I surrendered to it, allowing the agony to wash over me, each wave carving out space for release and understanding. As I purged into a bucket, I felt the release, freeing me from what I had carried for far too long.

I began to see my fears personified, standing before me like specters of my past. The fear of abandonment, the fear of not being enough, the fear of opening my heart again—each one wearing a face I recognized, each one representing the stories I had clung to for so long. I had thought I had buried them deep, but here they were, raw and inescapable.

As the night deepened, I realized that I was being invited to dance with these fears, to confront them rather than flee. I felt the presence of the shamans guiding us, their energy intertwining with the medicine, creating a safe space where we could explore the depths of our souls. They moved quietly among us, singing words of healing, reminding us it was okay to feel, to let the emotions flow without judgment or attaching ourselves to the story.

With every note they sang, I felt the burdens lift, as though the lyrics were healing my soul. I abandoned myself to the experience, each tear I shed a release of everything I had held inside unknowingly. The tears transformed into a river, a cathartic flow that washed away the pain I had carried for so long. I felt lighter, as if each drop took with it a piece of the burden I had been clinging to. In this surrender, I found my strength, remembering that healing does not come from avoiding pain but from embracing it. A profound sense of interconnectedness filled me, a reminder that we are all part of something greater than ourselves. The lessons of the plants began to seep into my consciousness, whispering truths I had once known but had long forgotten.

As the first light of dawn crept in, I took a deep breath, feeling a strange mixture of exhaustion and pride wash over me. The night had been intense. I had traversed through the landscape of my soul, facing my shadows and embracing my fears. It was hard to put into words, but I felt lighter somehow, as if my past was now truly behind me. In the stillness that followed, as we gathered our thoughts and shared our experiences, I understood that this was not just a ceremony; it was a celebration of life, of love, and of the infinite possibilities that lay ahead. I had taken a step deeper into my own healing, but unlike the two years during which I had worked on myself in solitude, this time the work was not done alone; we are all navigating this path together.

Stepping outside, I was met by the fresh embrace of the morning air. The world around me was slowly waking up, the sound of nature blending with the distant sounds of life beginning again. I could feel the Bali sun's warmth spreading across my skin, a gentle reminder that each new day carries the possibility of renewal, only this time with more awareness. It's because of these hard moments of stepping into the unknown to heal that I now view my past not as a chain of suffering, but as a series of lessons, each a moment that shaped my growth.

We all have those moments, don't we? The ones where pain feels like it's never going to let us go. I want you to know something: The power to heal has always been yours. The choice to release, to reclaim yourself, is yours to make, even if you haven't fully embraced it yet. You can choose how to respond to the remnants of old wounds, instead of letting them control you. Those triggers? They are invitations—opportunities for you to rewrite your responses, to reclaim the strength you may have spent so long surrendering. Healing isn't about forgetting; it's about choosing, again and again, to rise. And it is in this act of rising, in claiming yourself, that you touch your sovereignty, that you recognize that you are a being of light—capable of embracing love, compassion, and strength in ways you may never have imagined.

CHAPTER 20

THE REST IS STILL UNWRITTEN

As I rode through the winding streets of Bali on my motorbike, a familiar song began to play in my headphones, and this time it resonated with a different intensity. I had heard these lyrics countless times, but today, they felt like a message meant for me. As "Unwritten" by Natasha Bedingfield played, I could feel it deep inside—a rush of clarity and possibility. It wasn't just a song—it was a reminder from the universe, a nudge telling me that my story was mine to tell, and this was only the beginning of another chapter.

I was approaching my thirtieth birthday, reflecting on the many versions of myself I had been in Bali over the past five years. The years had been filled with growth, heartache, resilience, and moments of deep, profound change. Each phase felt like a distinct chapter in a book, one where I transformed over and over again. I had been the lost girl sharing her life on social media, attempting to piece together an identity through filtered images and fleeting validation. I had been the fitness bodybuilding coach that people aspired to look like, sculpting not just my body but my sense of self-worth around external ideals. And I had been the heartbroken woman, raw and unraveling, struggling to make sense of the pain that felt as if it would never end. Even though we are all in this together, the truth is no one could speak my words for me. We each walk our own unique path, and I've come to understand that we're all connected through the stories we live. It's in hearing our story in the voices of others, through lyrics, poems, and shared experiences, that we find ourselves mirrored back, even in the darkest times. Where I once sought comfort, now I find insight and the recognition that while our stories are different, the emotions, the struggles, and the triumphs are universal.

But despite these reflections, there was a part of me still clinging to something I couldn't quite name. As my thirtieth birthday loomed closer, I found myself wrestling with the concept of aging, a quiet panic stirring within me. Was I leaving behind the best parts of myself? Had I missed some hidden milestone, some moment where life was supposed to make sense?

Aging is a curious thing. It doesn't happen all at once; it sneaks up on you in the small, quiet moments. At twenty, thirty feels like some distant shore, a place where you'll arrive polished, certain, and whole. But as I neared that milestone, I realized that turning thirty wasn't about reaching a destination—it was more about acceptance. Letting go of the illusion that we are ever meant to have everything figured out. Sabrina, my close friend, had a way of seeing through me, calling me out, and speaking the truth. That late September afternoon, we were tucked under the shade of a Bali café, sipping iced coffee, watching the world go by, when I opened up to her about the unease creeping in as my birthday approached.

"I don't know why, but it feels like time is slipping away," I admitted, brushing back a strand of hair. "Thirty, Sabrina. It feels like…that's old, right?"

She raised an eyebrow, giving me one of her signature looks—the look that always called out my nonsense without saying a word. "Old?" She leaned forward, her voice soft but firm. "Who told you that? This—right now—this is where life starts, not some expiration date set by the world."

Her words landed heavier than I expected. She was right, of course. I had been clinging to the societal conditioning that taught women to fear aging, to dread the loss of youth as if it meant losing our value. But Sabrina's conviction, her belief that life was just beginning for me, was a powerful paradigm shift for me. My fear of turning thirty wasn't just the number, but about everything it represented—the transition from the innocence of youth to the wisdom of experience. The shift I felt was less about age itself and more about transitioning from the maiden to the mother archetype. It wasn't literal for me, since I was not about to become a mother, but there was a shift in energy, settling into my own skin that hadn't been there before.

The maiden, with her innocence and wide-eyed wonder, had fulfilled her purpose. I could see the reflection of who I had once been, yet she no longer matched the woman I was becoming. There was a grounded energy to this new phase, a sense of strength that came not from the endless pursuit of validation but from wisdom earned through navigating life's unpredictable path. I found myself mourning the loss of my youthful idealism but also embracing the quiet power that came with experience. It was the merging of the dreamer and the doer, the idealist and the realist, as if all the pieces of myself were finally coming together.

After my conversation with Sabrina, I found myself smiling as I thought about the chapters I had yet to write, the parts of myself I had yet to discover. Life is always a work in progress, constantly inviting us to step deeper into the unknown. In those moments of doubt and uncertainty, it's the whispers of the universe—through a song, a friend's words, or a moment of stillness—that remind us to keep moving forward. My birthday was simply where my book continued, and each day that followed was an opportunity to write it with more courage, more love, and more truth than ever before.

Life is a cycle of beginnings and endings, and through it all, we are always authoring our stories. I used to think that life was linear—point A to point B, one milestone leading naturally to the next. But over time, I realized life is far more cyclical, with each chapter enriching the next. Where we're headed may matter, but what matters even more are the choices we make along the way, the lessons we learn, the journey we take. Setting goals and envisioning the future is important, but I've come to believe that those goals can only truly align when they come from a place of inner knowing—a soul-level alignment with who we are, before the world told us who to be.

In my late teens and early twenties, I set countless goals for myself. Some of them were the kind you'd expect—a career that seemed aspirational, a fitness regimen that would make me feel strong, relationships that offered validation. I was working hard to build an image of success that matched the ideals I had absorbed from society, from Instagram, from the people around me. But when I reached those milestones, I was left feeling emptier than I expected. I had worked so hard to become someone, but I wasn't sure if that someone was really me.

When I started to strip back the layers (and it took a long time to even realize I needed to), I saw that much of my life had been shaped by external expectations. There was this narrative I was trying to fit into—who I should be, what I should look like, how I should live my life. None of those things were truly mine. They were borrowed ideas, projections from a world that didn't understand the intricacies of my heart, my fears, my desires. And that holds true for so many of us. We walk around with these hand-me-down dreams, trying to live up to some invisible standards, and all the while, our own voice gets quieter and quieter.

In those moments of confusion, like my time trapped in a toxic cycle with Ryan, it wasn't that I had lost my way entirely; it was that I had stopped listening to my inner voice—the one that knew, deep down, what I was capable of and where I was meant to go. It made me realize that setting goals isn't about achieving external success or reaching some destination society has mapped out for us. It's about aligning those goals with who we are at our core, before the world told us who to be.

I started to think differently about my future. Instead of focusing on what I thought I should want, I began to ask myself what my soul truly craved. I asked myself what kind of life I wanted to live—not just the achievements, but the way I wanted to feel, the kind of person I wanted to be, the energy I wanted to carry.

It's a powerful thing when you align your goals with your soul. Suddenly, the steps you take aren't just oriented toward survival or success, but toward living in a way that feels deeply authentic to you. It's not easy, though. When you start to carve out your own path, doubts creep in. Impostor syndrome can hit hard, especially when you're stepping into something new, something that feels bigger than anything you've done before.

I've been there so many times. You make progress, you start to feel like you're really onto something, and then that voice in the back of your head whispers, "Who do you think you are?" It's like all the fears you've ever had about not being good enough come rushing in. But I've learned that those moments are a sign that you're moving in the right direction. Growth feels uncomfortable because you're stretching beyond what you've known. The fear, the uncertainty, they're all part of the process. And the only way to push through it is to trust that you're capable, even when you don't feel like it.

One of the most important lessons I've learned is to listen to the nudges from the universe. We often expect our path to be laid out in some clear step-by-step plan, but life rarely works like that. Sometimes the guidance we need comes in whispers—a chance conversation, a book falling into our hands at the right moment, an unexpected opportunity. It's easy to ignore those signs when we're caught up in the chaos of life, but when we slow down and pay attention, we start to see that the universe is always guiding us.

Here's the thing—sometimes, you *will* get lost. Sometimes, despite your best intentions, you'll find yourself off track, unsure of what to do next. That is part of the journey. It's easy to get frustrated in those moments, to feel like you've failed. But I've come to believe that getting lost is just another way of finding yourself. When you lose your way, it forces you to slow down, to reassess, to ask yourself what really matters. And when you come back to your heart, when you listen to that quiet voice within, you'll find your way again.

For a long time, I struggled to accept help from others. I thought I had to do everything on my own, and that asking for help was a sign of weakness. But the truth is, we're not meant to walk this path alone. People come into our lives for a reason, and sometimes they hold the key to something we need, something we can't unlock on our own. Whether it's a word of encouragement, a piece of advice, or even just someone holding space for us, other people can be the bridge that helps us get to where we're meant to be.

You don't have to have all the answers, and you don't need to be fearless. Fear will always be present in some form, but it doesn't have to control you. The key is to feel the fear and take the step anyway. Visualizing the life you want for yourself is the first step. But it's not enough to just imagine it—you have to take action. Even small steps, even when you're unsure, even when you're afraid. This could mean moving. Breaking off a bad relationship. Quitting a job that is hindering you. The universe meets us where we are, and when we show up with intention and a willingness to move forward, doors begin to open.

I went searching for answers in places where few dare to tread. I sought wisdom from those who had walked the path before me, sitting at the feet of masters and bowing my head in reverence at altars heavy with the weight of ancient knowledge. I was searching, unsure of what I was truly seeking, yet driven by a longing for healing and understanding. Part of me was yearning to break free from the suffocating grip of my own thoughts, the heaviness of grief and self-doubt that felt like chains around my spirit.

There was one medicine ceremony, in particular, where I found myself lost in confusion. I had anticipated a grand journey, visions dancing before my eyes, revelations awakening knowledge I hadn't yet realized I carried. Instead, I felt like a ghost, haunting the fringes of my own experience, searching for a connection that seemed just out of reach. In my frustration and confusion, I humbly laid my truth bare before the Colombian shaman. "I don't know why I keep coming back," I confessed, my voice soft yet pained. "I don't know what I'm searching for anymore."

He paused, his gaze dropping to the altar, his brow furrowing like he was searching for the answer not just for me, but for himself as well. In that moment, it was as though I were inside my own heart. Then, as if the medicine or spirit had whispered the words into his soul, he spoke the one thing I had been yearning to hear: "Freedom."

That single word was medicine. I began to weep as he played the drum and served me peyote. This sacred cactus worked its way into me gradually, a slow, steady presence that radiated from my core outward. Its energy was patient and deliberate, grounding me while simultaneously opening my heart and mind. With each heartbeat, it guided me inward, gently revealing the habits, fears, and attachments I had been clutching and showing me where I had been resisting my own truth. It wasn't forceful or overwhelming—it simply held space for me to meet myself fully. There's a profound freedom that comes with embracing your authentic self, with peeling away the layers of who you thought you had to be to reveal the vibrant essence of who you truly are. It's not about running away from who you've become; it's about returning to the essence of what has always been there, buried beneath the chaos and noise of life.

So, as you navigate your own path, I encourage you to do the same. Reflect on where you've been, honor the lessons you've learned, and use them as fuel to create the future you desire. Trust your intuition, take bold steps in the direction of your dreams, and remember: Even when you feel lost, you are never truly off course. The universe has a way of guiding us back to where we're meant to be, as long as we keep moving forward with an open heart and a willingness to embrace what life places before us.

I don't know where I am going or what the destination looks like, and I have no idea who I might meet along the way. Truthfully, it feels a little bit scary. But I know I have myself, my skills, and the people around me who love me, along with a deep understanding of my soul. I trust in something much greater than myself to guide and support me, while also recognizing my own strength. I've made it this far, and I will continue to believe that wherever my soul leads me is exactly where I am meant to be.

And you? You too can trust your path. Even when the way ahead seems shrouded in uncertainty, remember that every choice you make is an integral part of your unique journey. Welcome the unexpected, for it is often in those moments that the most profound growth occurs. Your experiences, both the joys and the challenges, are shaping you into who you are meant to become, so listen to your heart; it knows the way. Trust that the detours are guiding you toward something beautiful and have faith in the timing of your life.

Your story is still unfolding, and the best part? You're not writing it alone—you're co-creating it with life itself. So, as cliché as it might sound, dream without limits, lean into trust, and remember that all you need already rests within you.

CHAPTER 21

THE SIGNIFICANCE OF OUR SCARS

There are moments in life that change us. They arrive without warning, carried in something as simple as a look, a word, or a shared silence. These are the moments that remind us why we've endured the hard seasons, why we've done the work to heal, why we've chosen not to give up on love, no matter how difficult life may have felt. I didn't know it at the time, but one of those moments was about to unfold.

The world around us faded into the background, the clinking of glasses and quiet murmurs of conversation dissolving as if they belonged to a distant reality. On our first date, as the plates between me and Mikel slowly emptied and our conversation stretched into the evening, we sat suspended in a space that felt untouched by time. It wasn't only a spark; there was a deeper connection I felt right away. There was a comfort in the silence between us, a recognition of something I couldn't quite place, but had been waiting for from a man.

With every laugh, every shared story, I found myself wanting to know more, to unravel the layers of who he was. There was something about Mikel that felt familiar, as if we had both been waiting for this moment long before it arrived. His energy matched mine, his depth mirrored my own, and it was as if Mikel saw me—not just the version of myself I showed to the world, but the woman beneath it, the one shaped by everything I had lived through.

That first date felt like a turning point, not just in meeting someone new, but in discovering new parts of myself. I had spent so long healing, rebuilding, guarding my heart with caution. I felt ready to let someone in—to let someone be a part of my world. The thought was overwhelming. How could I trust someone with my heart again after it had been shattered? How do you believe in something that has so often left you empty? But as I sat across from Mikel, watching the way he looked at me like he already understood, I realized that love is a risk you have to take, no matter how many times it leaves you broken.

To truly love someone means allowing them to see the scars, the past wounds that shaped you, the parts of yourself you have tried to hide. It's about standing in front of them, unguarded, and saying, *"This is me—can you love me still?"* Love is never without risk. It asks you to open up to the possibility of heartbreak, to step into the unknown, knowing full well it might not end the way you hope but choosing to dive in anyway. And with the right person, I wanted that. I wanted my partner to see me—the healed parts and the broken ones. The pieces I was proud of and the ones I was still learning to accept. The heart, fragile yet resilient, yearns to be known, to be understood, and to be loved—not in spite of its flaws but because of them. And I knew if I wanted something real, I couldn't keep hiding behind the walls I had built to protect myself. I had to tear them down.

But opening up after years of self-preservation felt like standing at the edge of a cliff, looking down at the drop, unsure if I would fall or if someone would catch me. As I began to speak my truth, to share the parts of my past, and particularly my history in the strip club, a familiar but deeply unsettling fear of rejection gripped my heart, threatening to overwhelm the courage I had spent so long cultivating. *What if everything goes terribly wrong? What if I ruin this before it has even begun?* The potential for rejection felt like a monumental risk, one that seemed to hang in the balance with every second that passed. But despite the fear, despite the overwhelming vulnerability, I knew in my heart that the time had come. I had spent too many years keeping people at a distance, too many moments choosing safety over connection. And so, with my heart in my hands, I took a breath and let him in.

"I worked in a strip club," I admitted, my voice soft but steady. His deep brown eyes, usually so full of charm and ease, now watched me intently, giving me the space to share the truth I had finally decided to reveal.

"I did it for the money," I continued, the words catching in my throat as I admitted the reality of my situation. "I didn't know what else to do, so I did the best I could."

The silence stretched between us as my anxiety amplified. My pulse quickened, but I held his gaze. Had I just shattered something between us? Had I said too much? What if my vulnerability had pushed him away, and he walked off without a word like Harry had done? I had taken a gamble, exposing a piece of myself that had stayed locked away for so long, a part of me that

I had long believed would never see the light of day again. But wasn't this what I had always wanted? To be truly seen? To be loved for all that I was? Yet I knew that to deepen a true connection with someone—if it was ever going to be real—required me to show up fully, without a mask.

I waited, heart open, my eyes fixed on his expression, searching for any sign of what would come next. His face, calm and steady as always, gave away nothing at first. Even as I waited for his response—though fear prickled at me—another part of me felt strangely empowered by my honesty. I knew that this moment was bigger than just his response. This wasn't just a turning point in our connection; it was a turning point for me. For so long, I had measured my worth by how others received me, by his reaction and whether I was accepted or rejected. And yet, his reaction, while incredibly important to me, no longer held the power it once had. I had started to unveil my past as if it were a confession, but it wasn't that at all. As I found the courage to speak about that part of myself and my story, what I experienced was an incredible victory. I had found the strength to speak my truth, regardless of the outcome, and I owned it in front of another human being. I had already won the most important battle I had ever faced: reclaiming not just my own story with its light and shadow, its mistakes and its achievements, but my own worth.

"Or at least, that's what I believed at the time." I finally said, picking the story back up, my words deliberate. "I'm not proud of it. But it's part of who I am, part of what made me the person sitting in front of you now. The good and the bad."

I dared another glance at Mikel, watching his expression, curious to see his reaction to the truth I was offering. His expression softened. Though his face remained hard to read, he reached across the table, his hand warm as it closed over mine. The gesture brought a steady reassurance—I had spoken my truth, and that was enough.

Years of living in survival mode, and then choosing to heal, had shaped a resilience I hadn't even known I possessed. Despite the fear of abandonment that had followed me like a shadow since childhood, I had learned to commit to living authentically. This moment was the culmination of years of struggling to embrace the parts of myself that I had been taught to believe were unworthy of love.

The memory of the first time I tried to share this part of myself with someone else came flooding back—Harry, my first love as an adult. I had felt suffocated with shame back then, like my very existence was a mistake and was ready for the world to swallow me whole. But now, years later, I understood a fundamental truth: To live authentically, that commitment to honesty must start with oneself.

The road to self-acceptance has been long and winding, fraught with moments of doubt and fear, and the occasional urge to retreat into the comfort of old versions of myself. I have stumbled more times than I can count, falling face-first into painful realizations that forced me to confront everything I had tried to outrun. The process of facing my past has been as excruciating as walking through the club's dim corridors in high heels, my feet throbbing with every step, and the weight of the choices I had to make peace with. But pain has a way of chiseling away at the parts of us that are not real. Each wound, each painful revelation, has added to my strength. The further I've walked, the more I've discovered about myself, peeling away layers of self-doubt and learning to stand taller, stronger.

When people hear that I worked as a stripper, they don't always look beyond their own preconceptions. They see stereotypes, the illusions they've been fed by society—a narrative that lacks nuance, humanity, and truth. There is a story the world tells about women like me, and it is not a kind one. The people who judge, the ones who dismiss with quiet disdain, rarely stop and ask how I got there, what I learned, or what it took to step into that world and, more importantly, to step out of it. They don't see the resilience it required, the depth of conversation held in dimly lit booths, the insights gained into human psychology, and the strength I had to build up to show up each night ready to face whatever came my way, all while balancing on stiletto heels. Through this life, I have developed an ability to see beyond the masks we wear, recognizing the hidden self we carry within. I have learned that our outward presentation often belies the complex inner worlds we inhabit, the hardships we've faced, and the strength it takes to navigate our daily lives.

Once imprisoned by shame, I now see my journey as a testament to the transformative power of human resilience. The very experiences that once threatened to break me have become the foundation of my healing. I've come to understand that my pain wasn't purposeless; it was the trial in which my strength was built. I share my story as a guiding light of hope, inviting others to see reflections of their own struggles in the journey of my past. The hurt, the betrayal, the disturbances, and the tragedies I've endured are not unique to me. They are the common threads that bind us all in our shared human experience. Through my story, I hope to illuminate the path to healing that is attainable for everyone, no matter how dark their present may seem.

In a world where we often wear masks of perfection, it's easy to forget that beneath the surface, each person carries their own invisible burdens. The stranger you pass on the street, the colleague you see every day—their hearts may be gripped by unseen traumas. Our tendency to hide our true selves behind masks of normalcy isolates us from each other, cutting us off from the connections that could help us heal as we all mirror one another. We all want to be seen for who we are, but we fear what others will think. The truth is, the only way forward is through the courage to be vulnerable. By revealing the parts of ourselves we've kept hidden, we invite others to do the same.

Our scars are not imperfections to be concealed; they are proof of survival, evidence of battles fought and won. Each one tells a story of a moment when we faced a challenge and overcame it, even if the victory was just making it to the next day. Strength is often misunderstood. To the outside world, it can look effortless, as if resilience was something we were born with rather than something we built through pain, doubt, and perseverance. But those of us who have walked through fire know the truth. We know the countless nights spent in tears, the sacrifices made, replaying choices we cannot change. We know the burden of sacrificing parts of ourselves just to make it through. These were once the untold chapters behind every smile, every achievement, and the invisible foundation upon which my life is built.

Pain, if we allow it, can be our greatest teacher. The trials I've endured now serve as my credentials. There is a certain irony in the way we hide the very things that others are desperately seeking—resilience under pressure, resourcefulness in scarcity, perseverance in adversity. It's time to make a decision: to recognize that the hardships we have defeated have qualified us for where we stand today. In ancient tales, warriors were recognized by their scars; the marks of violence on their flesh were a physical manifestation of their bravery in battle. Yet, in our modern world, we are told to cover them, to act as if our struggles never existed. But what if we didn't? What if, instead of treating our past as something to be ashamed of, we saw it as a roadmap to survival for others who are fighting their own wars? Your story isn't merely for your validation; it's for initiation and an invitation for others to keep going, to believe that there is life on the other side of pain.

To truly heal, we must first allow ourselves to acknowledge the hurt and be vulnerable enough to show our true selves. In doing so, we don't just liberate ourselves; we become a guide for those still finding their way through the darkness. I remember moments when giving up seemed like the only option and when ending it all felt like it would be a release. But my story, the one I believed would end in despair, now stands as proof of what happens when we choose to stay. The joy, the growth, the rebirth—it all exists on the other side of choice. This is the alchemy of healing, the transformation of wounds into scars, and scars into wisdom.

Life's journey is filled with challenges that threaten to break us, from job loss to toxic relationships and the death of loved ones. And while we don't always have control over what happens to us, we do have control over what we choose to do with it. Our wounds need not remain open forever. They can be tended to, cared for, and eventually closed—not erased, but integrated into who we are. The first step is to acknowledge them, to stop numbing and suppressing, and instead listen to what they are trying to tell us. Our mind communicates with our heart, and our heart connects with our spirit. Ignoring the hurt only spreads its poison to other parts of our lives. Resentment, secret addictions, and anger at circumstances all serve as things that will never soothe the pain. True healing is not found in denying what has broken us but in facing it, understanding it, and choosing, day by day, to move forward despite it.

It is crucial to distinguish between a healing wound and a closed scar. A wound remains tender, vulnerable to the slightest trigger, easily reopened by a familiar song, an unexpected memory, or a fleeting encounter that brings the past rushing back to perpetuate the cycle of pain. But a scar? A scar is the mark of completed healing. It allows us to carry our experiences without being crippled by them. Yes, the pain was real. Yes, there was a season of affliction. But you're still here, still alive and still evolving. A scar shows the completion of the journey. You can carry your past, but it no longer dictates your future.

True healing is evident when intrusive thoughts no longer steal our peace, when old wounds no longer weigh heavily on our hearts, when old memories no longer feel like open doors to suffering but rather chapters, then we have finished reading. The scars we bear may not always be visible, but they hold power nonetheless. It is why we have a duty to carry their stories with our words, to write the way forward for those who need it most. By sharing our past, we form a powerful constellation of human connection, each one of us like a star in the sky, guiding lost travelers home. Let's shine brightly with our scars, navigate our unique journeys, and illuminate the way for others. In our willingness to be seen, we find our true north, and through our shared celestial map, we discover the universe that connects us all.

In the dance between shadow and light, in the space between reality and fantasy, in the silent moments between heartbeats, that is where transformation unfolds. It is in these in-between moments, where reality blurs with longing, where we confront both our fears and our deepest desires, that we discover who we truly are. It is here, in the raw and unfiltered depths of self-exploration, that the real magic happens. With each step forward on this cosmic journey of self-discovery, I feel myself unraveling and expanding all at once, shedding versions of myself that no longer fit and stepping into something greater than I ever imagined. What began in a dimly lit club was never just about survival or seduction; it was an initiation. An invitation to understand what it truly means to be a woman—not just in the way the world defines her, but in the way she learns to define herself. In all her contradictions, complexities, and untamed magnificence, she exists fully. And in finding her, I have found myself.

ACKNOWLEDGMENTS

First, to the women who have walked through shadows, carried unspoken stories, and questioned their worth, thank you for showing me the depth, courage, and resilience of the human spirit. You are the heart of this book.

To the women who have worked in the club, you know the weight of being seen and unseen all at once. Your strength, your survival, your refusal to be diminished by judgment taught me what real power looks like. This book exists because of what you carry and what you've overcome.

To Jenna, my agent, who saw what this book could become before I did and fought to bring it into the world, your belief changed everything. To the team at Post Hill Press, who handled these stories with care and gave them a home, thank you for your trust and your vision.

To the mentors, guides, and teachers who shared their wisdom so generously, and to the countless writers whose words gave me courage when I had none, I am endlessly grateful for your example. To my friends and family, who believed in me when I needed the push to believe in myself, thank you for holding me through every chapter.

To the lands of Bali, where stillness taught me patience, and to the city of London, where energy and chaos reminded me of my edges, thank you for holding me and my work in your arms.

And above all, to the woman brave enough to pick up this book and strip herself back to her soul, thank you. This is for you.

ABOUT THE AUTHOR

Jade Marrey is a transformational co-ach, podcast host, writer, and speaker whose journey of self-discovery has inspired women across the world. Raised between the UK and Ireland and now based in Bali, Jade is known for her raw honesty, spiritual depth, and ability to make personal growth feel intimate and real. Her work explores themes of self-worth, feminine energy, shadow work, and radical self-acceptance.

Jade's viral empowerment videos have reached millions, building a global community drawn to her soulful, relatable voice. Her podcast, *Stripped to the Soul*, attracts thousands of monthly listeners, offering unfiltered conversations on healing, growth, and stepping into your fullest self.

Through her content, coaching, and storytelling, Jade creates a powerful space for women to peel back the layers, break free from societal conditioning, and remember who they were before the world told them who to be.